CHINESE
FOLKTALES
FOR LANGUAGE LEARNERS

中国传统民间故事

CHINESE FOLKTALES

FOR LANGUAGE LEARNERS

Famous Folk Stories in Chinese and English

Vivian Ling & Wang Peng

Illustrated by Yang Xi

TUTTLE Publishing

Tokyo | Rutland, Vermont | Singapore

About the Authors

Vivian Ling has enjoyed a long career teaching Chinese language and literature at Oberlin College and Indiana University, and directing language programs in Taipei, Shanghai, Kunming and Beijing. She is the author of many books, including *The Field of Chinese Language Education in the U.S.: A Retrospective of the 20th Century*. She has also co-authored several books with Wang Peng, including *Essential Mandarin Chinese Grammar*, *Chinese Stories for Language Learners*, *A Bilingual Treasury of Chinese Folktales* and *The Twelve Animals of the Chinese Zodiac*.

Wang Peng has been on the faculty at Georgetown University since 2002, teaching Chinese language courses at many levels. Formerly, she was chief instructor at the Inter-University Program for Chinese Language Studies of Tsinghua University, and taught Chinese at Oberlin College and Brown University. This is the fifth book she has co-authored with Vivian Ling.

About the Illustrator

Yang Xi is an art teacher at Qingdao Huanghai University. Her distinctive style incorporates classical and contemporary Chinese and Western influences. She holds an MA degree from the College of Fine Arts at Nanjing Art Institute.

Contents

A Message to Readers   7

The Chinese Story of Creation 华夏民族的创世纪   10

The Divine Agriculturist and Pioneer of Herbal Medicine
神农尝百草   24

Tamer of the Great Floods 大禹治水   38

The Invention of Chinese Writing 仓颉造字   52

How Silk was Invented 丝绸女神嫘祖   66

Lu Ban the Master Craftsman and Builder 鲁班的传说   78

Two Virtuous Mothers of Ancient China 慈母与虎妈   92

The Virtuous Wife 乐羊子妻   104

Peace Consort Wang Zhaojun 昭君出塞   118

An Emperor's Comfort Food 珍珠翡翠白玉汤   134

Taming the New Year's Beast 年兽的故事   148

China's Romeo and Juliet 梁山伯与祝英台   162

A Young Widow's Sorrow 孟姜女哭长城   178

Judge Bao Takes On the Emperor's Son-in-Law
包公怒斩陈世美   192

The Ten Trials of a Taoist Sage 钟离权十考吕洞宾   208

Andio Tracklist and Their Text (Chinese) References

		Pages
01A.mp3	The Chinese Story of Creation 华夏民族的创世纪	11
01B. mp3	The Chinese Story of Creation_Historical Background 历史背景	17
02A.mp3	The Divine Agriculturist and Pioneer of Herbal Medicine 神农尝百草	25
02B.mp3	The Divine Agriculturist and Pioneer of Herbal Medicine_Postscript 后记	31
03A.mp3	Tamer of the Great Floods 大禹治水	39
03B.mp3	The Tamer of the Great Floods_Afterword 附录	45
04A.mp3	The Invention of Chinese Writing 仓颉造字	53
04B.mp3	The Invention of Chinese Writing_Afterword 附录	59
05A.mp3	How Silk Was Invented 丝绸女神嫘祖	67
05B.mp3	How Silk Was Invented_Afterword 附录	71
06A.mp3	Lu Ban the Master Craftsman and Builder 鲁班的传说	79
06B.mp3	Lu Ban the Master Craftsman and Builder_Afterword 附录	85
07A.mp3	Two Virtuous Mothers of Ancient China 慈母与虎妈	93
07B.mp3	Two Virtuous Mothers of Ancient China_Afterword 附录	99
08A.mp3	The Virtuous Wife 乐羊子妻	105
08B.mp3	The Virtuous Wife_Commentary 评论	111
09A.mp3	Peace Consort Wang Zhaojun 昭君出塞	119
09B.mp3	Peace Consort Wang Zhaojun_Afterword 附录	127
10A.mp3	An Emperopr's Comfort Food 珍珠翡翠白玉汤	135
10B.mp3	An Emperopr's Comfort Food_Commentary 评论	143
11A.mp3	Taming the New Year's Beast 年兽的故事	149
11B.mp3	Taming the New Year's Beast_Afterword 附录	155
12A.mp3	China's Romeo and Juliet 梁山伯与祝英台	163
12B.mp3	China's Romeo and Juliet_Afterword 附录	169
13A.mp3	A Young Widow's Sorrow 孟姜女哭长城	179
13B.mp3	A Young Widow's Sorrow_Commentary 评论	185
14A.mp3	Judge Bao Takes on the Emperor's Son-in-Law 包公怒斩陈世美	193
14B.mp3	Judge Bao Takes on the Emperor's Son-in-Law_Afterword 附录	201
15A.mp3	The Ten Trials of a Taoist Sage 钟离权十考吕洞宾	209
15B.mp3	The Ten Trials of a Taoist Sage_Afterword 附录	219

A Message to Readers

Welcome to the land of Chinese folklore, a delightful corner of the Chinese heritage that remains relatively unexplored in Western publications. This book is intended to lead readers from other parts of the world into this corner of the Chinese heritage and share with them some of its best treasures. Even though this is a bilingual book, you need not be bilingual to enjoy the folklore presented here. In fact, you may not know any Chinese at all, but after delving into this book, you just might be inspired to begin learning Chinese, so that you can explore Chinese culture and engage with Chinese people in greater depth.

A second purpose of this book, equally important as the first, is to provide Chinese language learners with a vehicle for enhancing the language learning experience. Mastering Chinese as a foreign language is a long and arduous journey that requires sustained motivation. But that journey can be turned into a fun adventure by incremental rewards and fascinating vistas along the way. If you are a learner of Chinese, we hope you will find in this book the motivating rewards to lighten up your journey. Language learning and cultural acquisition are mutually reinforcing. They are in fact two legs that work in tandem. We hope this book will show you how these two legs cooperate at their best, and help you discover the joy of this learning journey.

Folklore is sometimes treated as "literature light" in academia, ranked a notch below the literary canon produced by literati for literati. As academics, we the authors have enjoyed delving into the traditional Chinese literary canon, but have come to see folklore as a delectable but under-appreciated part of the Chinese literary heritage. It is folklore that shines a light on the culture of the nameless common folks, the unsung heroes on whose backs Chinese civilization was built.

Until the mid-20th century, literacy was the privilege of the elite minority of the Chinese population. The culture and entertainment of the common people were conveyed through the medium of storytelling and the performing arts, and this is where folklore flourished. These stories are about universal human concerns such as the origin of humankind, impact of wars and natural disasters, legendary cultural heroes, dignity and justice for the common folks, and yearnings of the human heart.

Folklore differs from the works of the literary canon in that it is organic and mutable, not frozen in time. To sustain the vitality of folktales, story tellers and performing artists tweaked the stories to make them relevant and meaningful to their audience, and that's why we have multiple versions of each folktale today. In writing this book, we have referenced the most widely accepted versions of these stories, but have also followed the tradition of the Chinese storytellers in highlighting aspects of the stories that are most meaningful to our contemporary cross-cultural audience. In this volume, each folktale is followed by a short essay about its historical context, relevance to other events in the history of China and elsewhere in the world, as well as to our contemporary world. In sum, our goal is to have this collection of interesting stories become a window into the history and culture of China.

While the stories in the English version may be enjoyed by readers with no Chinese language background, the bilingual format and the accompanying vocabulary lists are an extra bonus for readers with varying levels of Chinese language proficiency. The vocabulary lists are pitched at the high-intermediate level. Words in the Chinese text that are listed in the vocabulary are underlined; those that appear in footnotes are listed at the end of the corresponding lists, with a prefix "fn" in the numbering. If you find your vocabulary to be below the threshold of the vocabulary lists, you may minimize frustration and maximize fun by reading through the whole story in English first, then return to read it in Chinese. This will allow you to make intelligent guesses for the unfamiliar Chinese vocabulary.

In addition, we recommend that you reinforce your reading comprehension by listening to the audio recordings, which can be downloaded free from the Tuttle website (see instructions below). Reading comprehension and listening comprehension can be enhanced by doing the two activities in conjunction or separately. We suggest that you try it both ways to see which way works best for you.

The final section of each chapter is a set of discussion questions, designed to stimulate further thoughts about the contemporary relevance of the folktales. These questions may also serve as prompts for Chinese language students to practice their oral discussion skills.

We are delighted to see you here, and hope that you will be entertained while being enlightened!

Vivian Ling	Wang Peng	Yang Xi
English author	Chinese co-author	Illustrator

How to access the audio recordings for this book:

1. Check to be sure you have an Internet connection.
2. Type the URL below into your web browser.

www.tuttlepublishing.com/chinese-folktales-for-language-learners

For support you can email us at info@tuttlepublishing.com.

The Chinese Story of Creation

In prehistoric times there was no sky and earth. The universe was just one undefined mass. Within this mass a giant by the name of Pan Gu had lain asleep for eighteen thousand years. One day he suddenly woke up to find himself plunged in total darkness. In a panic he grabbed a hatchet and swung it at the dark nothingness. "Huala!" the nothingness split open, the part above the crack slowly rose to form the sky, the part below gradually fell to become the earth.

To prevent the earth and sky from merging again, Pan Gu stood tall with his feet firmly planted on the earth and his arms holding up the sky. Every day the sky continued to rise, and Pan Gu continued to grow taller. Finally, the earth and sky became stable, and Pan Gu collapsed from exhaustion.

From this time on, Pan Gu's body continued to transform into various earthly elements. His breath became the winds and clouds, his voice became roaring thunder, his eyes became the sun and the moon, his four limbs became the four cardinal directions, his skin spread out to form plains, his blood became flowing rivers, even his sweat became the rain that nourished a myriad of plants. That's how the natural world was created.

Eons later the goddess Nü Wa came into this world. But she found it to be a lonely place, as though something was missing.

华夏民族的创世纪

在远古时代，天地还没有分开，宇宙还是一团混沌。一个名叫盘古的巨人在这团混沌中沉睡了一万八千年。有一天，盘古突然醒过来了，发现自己困在一片漆黑当中。盘古拿起一把斧头，左砍右劈。"哗啦"一声巨响，这团漆黑突然分开了，慢慢上升的一片变成了天，渐渐下沉的一片变成了地。

为了永久地把天地分开，盘古双脚牢牢地站在地上，双臂高高举起撑着天。天一天天升高，盘古也一日日长大。终于有一天，天地稳固了，盘古也筋疲力尽地倒在了地上。

后来，盘古的身体慢慢地变成了世间万物。他呼出的气息变成了风和云、他的声音变成了隆隆的雷鸣、他的眼睛变成了太阳和月亮、四肢变成了东西南北四个方向、皮肤变成了平原大地、血液变成了川流不息的江河、甚至他的汗水都变成了滋润万物的雨露。盘古就这样创造了自然界。

很久很久以后，女娲来到了这个世界上，不过她觉得很孤单，好像生活里缺少了一些东西。

One day when Nü Wa was feeling miserable because she was still lonely, she came to a pond and saw her reflection in the water. When she smiled, the image smiled back; when she pretended to frown, the image frowned too! This gave her an idea. She grabbed some mud from the riverbank and shaped it into a doll that looked just like herself. As soon as she stood the doll up, it started hopping around. Then it looked up at Nü Wa and called "Mama!" Suddenly, Nü Wa felt that she would never be lonely again! She knew that she had created a miracle, and she named it Ren.

　　有一天，女娲又因为感到孤单而非常难过。她来到一个池塘边，在水中看见了自己的影子。她笑一笑，影子也冲着她笑一笑；她假装皱一皱眉，影子也跟她一样皱一皱眉！这时，女娲突然有了个主意。她从河岸上抓起了一把泥，捏了一个看上去像自己一样的小娃娃。她刚把小娃娃放到地上，小娃娃就跳来跳去，抬起头看着女娲叫了一声"妈妈！"女娲立刻感到永远都不再孤单了！她知道自己创造了奇迹，于是把小娃娃叫作"人"。

Nü Wa was no longer lonely, but one Ren was not enough; she wanted to make more Rens and spread them all over the world. Day after day Nü Wa worked on this task. But no matter how hard she worked she couldn't make enough Rens to fill the whole world.

One day when she was outside working, it started to rain, and the ground became muddy and slippery. As she walked up a slope, she grabbed a vine to steady herself, but the vine broke and she fell. The vine then swung in the air and flung muddy droplets in all directions. As the droplets landed on the ground, they immediately came to life, just like Ren, except much smaller. They all started hopping around and calling "Mama! Mama! Mama!" Nü Wa was so happy she started to cry!

Over the next few days Nü Wa used the vine to quickly make many more Rens. But a new worry came over her. She knew that all the Rens would eventually die, and she would have to keep making more. Then she thought of an idea. She separated the Rens into two groups and told one group that they were boys and the other group that they were girls. Then she told them that when they grew up, they would create more Rens like themselves.

Finally, having reassured herself that mankind would perpetuate themselves, Nü Wa let out a big yawn and lay down to catch up on much-needed sleep. But just as she dozed off, she was awakened by thunderclaps. Rubbing her eyes, she saw lightning all around her, followed shortly by flames on mountain ridges that caught on fire. What happened next was even more horrendous—the sky cracked open, and torrential rain descended to earth, threatening to drown all the Rens who had only just settled down to live happily ever after.

女娲不再孤单了，但是只造一个人是远远不够的。女娲希望造更多的人，让全世界都有人！她开始每天造人，但是不管她多么努力，还是无法给全世界造出足够的人。

有一天，女娲正在外面造人，天下起了雨，地面变得泥泞湿滑。女娲爬上一面山坡，抓住了一条树藤，但是树藤突然断了，女娲也摔倒了。这时候，断掉的树藤飞到了空中，上面的泥巴点点落了一地。这些泥巴点点一落地就突然活了起来，看上去就像女娲造的人一样，只是个头更小一点儿。这些小人人围着女娲跳来跳去，口里叫着"妈妈！妈妈！妈妈！"看到这个景象，女娲高兴地哭了起来！

在接下来的几天里，女娲用那条树藤造了许许多多的人。不过她又有了一件心事儿。女娲知道所有的人总有一天会死的，那她就得不停地造人。这时候，女娲想到了一个主意。她把所有的人分成了两组，一组作为男孩儿，另一组作为女孩儿，并告诉他们长大以后，要一起合作造出像他们自己一样的人。

女娲相信，人类从那以后就会不断地自我繁衍了。这时候，她打了个哈欠，预备好好地补一补觉。女娲迷迷糊糊地刚要睡着，就被一声巨雷惊醒了。女娲揉揉眼睛一看，周边电闪雷鸣，很快附近的山脊上火焰冲天。接下来令人更惊恐的事情发生了——天空裂开了一个大窟窿，大雨倾盆而下，可能会淹死那些刚刚在这片土地上安居乐业的人！

Nü Wa knew instinctively that she had to seal the crack in the sky. The only glue strong enough to do the job was made by melting precious stones in five different colors. It took her nine days of searching in the nearby mountains and gullies to find all five precious stones. She carried the stones to the top of the highest mountain and dug a hole, in which she placed the stones, then started a fire to melt them. After another nine days, the stones finally transformed into molten steel. With no time to waste, she whisked a big banana leaf in the molten steel and flung it toward the cracked sky. A stream of light flashed toward the hole in the sky, then with a "snap-snap-snap," the crack was sealed!

Having been rescued from their first natural disaster, mankind returned to their peaceful life, though no one knows if they will live happily ever after. What we do know is that the Chinese people will forever remember Nü Wa as the goddess who created them and has looked after their well-being ever since.

Historical Background

The above Chinese story of creation is a composite of two separate myths, one about how the world was created, the other about how mankind came to be. We do not know when or how these myths began, but they must have circulated orally for many generations before they appeared in written records. In every story of creation, the natural world existed before humankind. Interestingly, the written records of China's two creation myths are dated in the reverse order.

出于<u>本能</u>，女娲觉得必须把天上的那个大窟窿补起来，而只有找到珍贵的五色石才有可能<u>炼石</u>补天。女娲花了九天九夜，走遍了附近的大山小沟，终于找齐了五色石。然后，她又把这些石头带到了最高的<u>山峰</u>上，<u>挖了一个坑</u>，将石头倒进坑里，燃火炼起了五色石。又过了九天九夜，珍贵的<u>石胶</u>终于炼成了。随后，女娲<u>操</u>起一枝巨大的<u>芭蕉叶</u>，将石胶<u>抛</u>向了那个大窟窿。只见一道亮光划过天空，飞向了大窟窿，又听见"啪啪啪"三声巨响之后，大窟窿终于补好了！

女娲<u>拯救</u>了人类，使他们<u>躲</u>过了第一次自然<u>灾害</u>。人们的生活又恢复了宁静，但谁也不知道未来还会发生什么。不过，中国人将永远<u>铭记</u>女娲是创造人类并<u>造福</u>他们的女神。

历史背景

这篇华夏民族的创世纪是两篇<u>神话</u>故事组合起来的，其中一篇说的是创世神话，而另一篇讲的是造人的故事。我们不太清楚这些神话故事<u>起源</u>的<u>确切</u>时间和背景，但这些故事一定是在有<u>文字记载</u>以前已经在民间以口头的形式<u>代代</u>相传了很久很久了。在不同文化的创世纪中，总是先有自然界，然后才有人类。有趣的是，中国的这两个神话，在文字记载的时间<u>顺序</u>上是正好相反的。

A written record of the Nü Wa story first appeared around the fourth century BCE, during the Warring States period, in the *Classic of Mountains and Seas*. This was a compilation of phenomenal accounts of the geography, culture, and legends of the known world at the time. As such, it is comparable to the present-day *National Geographic* magazine.

It was not until seven centuries later, during the Three Kingdoms period (221–265 CE), that Pan Gu was first mentioned in a written work. Even this work, *History of the Three Sovereigns and Five Emperors*, is no longer extant. However, the description of Pan Gu makes it clear that he was a fabricated mythical figure rather than a prehistoric human.

In contrast to Pan Gu, Nü Wa has all the characteristics of a human being, except that she performed certain superhuman feats. So, could she have been a historical person who was later glorified into a legend? This is plausible, because in another story Nü Wa supposedly coupled with the legendary Fu Xi and together they procreated humankind.

There is also some tenuous meteorological evidence to support the story of Nü Wa patching the cracked sky. Modern scientific studies have revealed a huge meteor shower four thousand to five thousand years ago, in which an enormous meteor struck north China, wreaking climatic havoc, and creating a humungous swamp. Could a historical Nü Wa have played a role in restoring the natural order? Apparently, many Chinese believe so. To this day there are many temples dotted across China dedicated to Nü Wa, the oldest and the most grandiose temple being the one in Handan, dating from 550 to 577 CE. However, Pan Gu is not entirely left out either, for there are also temples dedicated to him here and there.

女娲的神话故事最早记载于战国时期（公元前四世纪）的《山海经》。这本著作的内容包罗万象，主要记载了那个时代著名的地理、文化以及传奇故事。从这方面来看，《山海经》就像今天美国的《国家地理》杂志一样。

盘古的故事直到七个世纪之后的三国时期才出现在文字记载中，而最早记录盘古故事的《三五历纪》如今也已失传了。不过，盘古显然是一个创作出来的神话人物，而不是一个史前的真实人物。

女娲的故事却不同于盘古神话，她有着所有人类的特征，只不过也有一些超人的能力。那么，女娲是不是历史上的一个真实人物，而后来被传奇化了呢？完全有可能，因为在另一个故事中，女娲与传说中的伏羲结为了夫妻，成为了人类的始祖。

此外，从气象学的角度来说，女娲补天的故事似乎也有一点历史依据。现代科学研究发现，发生在4000–5000年前的一次大范围的流星雨当中，一颗巨大的陨石击中了中国北方，造成一场前所未有的天灾与特大洪涝灾害。当时是不是有一位名叫女娲的历史人物拯救了老百姓呢？显然许多中国人相信这是事实。直到现在，中国仍有不少地方还保留着祭拜女娲的寺庙，其中最古老、也是规模最大的就是公元550–577年建造在今日河北省邯郸市的女娲庙。不过，人们也没有忘记盘古，不少地方也能看到纪念盘古的寺庙。

Vocabulary

1. 华夏 **Huáxià** a historical word for China

2. 宇宙 **yǔzhòu** universe

3. 混沌 **hùndùn** primeval chaos

4. 盘古 **Pángǔ** Chinese mythological creator of universe

5. 困 **kùn** to be trapped in

6. 漆黑 **qīhēi** pitch dark

7. 斧头 **fǔtóu** hatchet

8. 左砍右劈 **zuǒkǎn yòupī** to swing (a sharp tool) right and left

9. 下沉 **xiàchén** to sink

10. 永久地 **yǒngjiǔde** permanently, forever

11. 牢牢地 **láoláode** firmly

12. 双臂 **shuāngbì** both arms

13. 撑 **chēng** to prop up

14. 稳固 **wěngù** stable, steady

15. 筋疲力尽 **jīnpí lìjìn** totally exhausted

16. 世间万物 **shìjiān wànwù** myriad things in the world

17. 气息 **qìxī** breath

18. 隆隆 **lónglóng** rumbling sound (onomatopoeia)

19. 雷鸣 **léimíng** sound of thunder

20. 四肢 **sìzhī** four limbs

21. 皮肤 **pífū** skin

22. 平原 **píngyuán** plain

23. 血液 **xuèyè** blood

24. 川流不息 **chuānliú bùxī** endlessly flowing rivers

25. 汗水 **hànshuǐ** perspiration

26. 滋润万物 **zīrùn wànwù** moisten or nourish myriad things

27. 雨露 **yǔlù** rain and dew

28. 女娲 **Nǚwā** Chinese mythological female figure

29. 孤单 **gūdān** lonely

30. 冲 **chòng** toward

31. 皱眉 **zhòuméi** to frown (lit. to knit the brow)

32. 池塘 **chítáng** pond

33. 捏 **niē** to knead with the fingers

34. 小娃娃 **xiǎo wáwa** small doll

35. 奇迹 **qíjì** miracle

36. 泥泞湿滑 **nínìng shīhuá** muddy and slippery

37. 山坡 **shānpō** mountain slope

38. 树藤 **shùténg** vines hanging from a tree

39. 摔倒 **shuāidǎo** to fall

40. 泥巴点点 **níbā diǎndiǎn** specks of mud

41. 个头 **gètóu** size (of a person or animal)

42. 景象 **jǐngxiàng** scenario

43. 心事儿 **xīnshìer** worry (lit. matter of the heart)

44. 繁衍 **fányǎn** to procreate

45. 打···哈欠 **dǎ... hāqiàn** to yawn

46. 补觉 **bǔjiào** to make up for lost sleep

47. 迷迷糊糊 **mímíhūhū** half awake, mind in a fog

48. 巨雷 **jùléi** huge thunder

49. 揉 **róu** to rub

50. 电闪雷鸣 **diànshǎn léimíng** lightning and thunder

51. 山脊 **shānjǐ** mountain ridge

52. 火焰冲天 **huǒyàn chōngtiān** flames rising to the sky

53. 惊恐 **jīngkǒng** terrified, panic-stricken

54. 裂开 **lièkāi** to crack open

55. 窟窿 **kūlong** hole

56. 倾盆而下 **qīngpén ér xià** to pour down like a tipped basin, downpour

57. 淹死 **yānsǐ** die from drowning

58. 安居乐业 **ānjū lèyè** to be well-settled in life and work

59. 本能 **běnnéng** instinctively

60. 炼石 **liànshí** to smelt rocks

61. 山峰 **shānfēng** mountain peak

62. 挖 **wā** to dig

63. 坑 **kēng** hole, pit

64. 石胶 **shíjiāo** molten rock

65. 操 **cāo** to grasp

66. 芭蕉叶 **bājiāoyè** banana leaf

67. 抛 **pāo** to toss

68. 拯救 **zhěngjiù** to rescue

69. 躲 **duǒ** to hide, to escape

70. 灾害 **zāihài** disaster

71. 铭记 **míngjì** to remember, to engrave on one's mind

72. 造福 **zàofú** to benefit

73. 神话 **shénhuà** myth, fairy tale

74. 起源 **qǐyuán** origin

75. 确切 **quèqiè** accurate, precise

76. 记载 **jìzǎi** to record (history)

77. 代代相传 **dàidài xiāngchuán** to transmit from generation to generation

78. 顺序 **shùnxù** order

79. 战国时期 **Zhànguó shíqī** Warring States period

80. 包罗万象 **bāoluó wànxiàng** to include everything, all-inclusive

81. 传奇 **chuánqí** legend

82. 三国时期 **Sānguó shíqī** Three Kingdoms period

83. 失传 **shīchuán** to be lost, no longer transmitted

84. 显然 **xiǎnrán** obviously

85. 特征 **tèzhēng** special characteristic

86. 超人 **chāorén** super-human

87. 伏羲 **Fúxī** a Chinese mythological figure

88. 气象学 **qìxiàngxué** meteorology

89. 角度 **jiǎodù** angle, perspective

90. 流星雨 **liúxīng yǔ** meteor shower

91. 陨石 **yǔnshí** meteor rock

92. 前所未有 **qiánsuǒwèiyǒu** unprecedented

93. 天灾 **tiānzāi** natural disaster

94. 洪涝 **hónglào** flood

95. 祭拜 **jìbài** to worship

96. 寺庙 **sìmiào** temple

97. 规模 **guīmó** scale, scope

98. 邯郸 **Hándān** a center of ancient Chinese civilization, presently a city in Hebei province

Questions for contemplation and discussion

I. Every culture has its own mythology of how the world and human-kind came to be. Can you compare the story of Genesis from the Judeo-Christian tradition, or another story of creation from your own culture, with the Chinese version in this chapter? Are there some universal similarities?

2. In your opinion, what are the human and superhuman characteristics of Nü Wa? What do you think is the significance of her super-human feats in the story?

3. Ancient China was a matrilineal society, as witnessed by the character "surname," composed of 女 "female" and 生 "born." It has also been suggested, but not proven, that China was also a matriarchal society. Do the two Chinese stories of creation shed any light on gender roles in ancient China?

4. Have you wondered why Chinese parents continue to tell these two creation stories to their children? What effect do you think they have on young formative minds?

5. Ask one or more Chinese friends to tell you their version of the Chinese creation story, and what they think about the story.

The Divine Agriculturist and Pioneer of Herbal Medicine

In a prehistoric time, well before China became China, humans in this part of the world were hunter-gatherers. Grains were indistinguishable from weeds and poisonous and medicinal plants grew side by side. No one knew which plants were edible, and which ones could be used to cure ailments. A certain tribal leader—one who was honored posthumously with the name Shen Nong, meaning "Divine Agriculturist"—was an exceptionally compassionate ruler. It pained him to see his people suffer from hunger and sickness, so he dedicated his life to ending this human misery.

Shen Nong knew he needed divine inspiration, so he secluded himself in the woods to meditate. On the third day a vision came to him: On the high mountains to the northwest there grew hundreds of plants unknown to mankind. It would be his job to find these plants and personally taste them to test their healing properties. The trek would be arduous and dangerous, but if he persevered, he would discover medicinal plants. With this vision, Shen Nong gathered a group of trusted followers and began their journey.

Within a few days Shen Nong and his followers developed blisters on their feet, and a few days later, the blisters turned to calluses. But the men persevered. After they had walked for forty-nine days, they finally saw a chain of mountain peaks in the distance. From afar, they could see many exotic flowers and grasses, and they could even faintly smell their fragrance. But as they walked on, this view seemed to move farther and farther away.

神农尝百草

上古时期，中原大地上还没有中国，那里的百姓都靠打猎、采野果为生。那时候，谷物和杂草混长在一起，毒草和草药也分不清。谁都不知道什么植物可以食用，哪些草药可以治病。有一位生后被人们尊称为"神农"的部落首领极富有同情心。看到百姓们挨饿，遭受病痛之苦，他十分悲伤，决心要为大家消灾祛病。

神农知道他需要得到神谕，于是就隐居在森林里苦思冥想。到了第三天，他终于有了主意：在西北方向的大山上，生长着几百种不为人知的野草。神农要去找到这些野草，并亲口尝一尝，试试它们的疗效。神农很清楚，这条路艰难又危险，但只要坚持，就一定能找到草药。有了这个目标，神农带领一队可以信赖的乡民们踏上了征程。

刚走了几天，神农和乡民们的脚都起了水泡，又走了几天，脚上的水泡已经成了老茧。但他们继续往前走。走啊，走啊，走了四十九天，终于看见了远方的一排山峰。他们远远地看见了一些奇花异草，也隐约闻见了花香。走着走着，那些山峰似乎离他们越来越远。

As Shen Nong led the group into the first valley, they were suddenly surrounded by a pride of leopards and tigers, as well as snakes! Shen Nong ordered the men to brandish their magic whips. After they had driven away the first group of beasts, another group surged toward them. For seven days and seven nights they fought off wave after wave of these beasts. Finally, they drove them all away. It is said that the stripes and spots on these beasts today are the scars from the thrashing they received. Having survived the battle against the beasts, Shen Nong's followers were in no mood to face another calamity, so they begged Shen Nong to turn back. Shen Nong shook his head and said, "How can we give up when our people are suffering from hunger and sickness?"

当神农领着大家走进第一条山谷时，突然窜出来一群豹子、老虎和蟒蛇，将他们团团围住了。神农立刻命令大家挥舞神鞭，把这群野兽赶走了。可是他们刚赶走了一群，又来了一群。就这样，他们跟那些野兽搏斗了七天七夜，终于把牠们全都赶走了。据说，现在老虎、豹子和蟒蛇身上的条纹和斑点就是当时被鞭打后留下的伤疤。跟野兽搏斗之后，乡民们都不想再继续前行了，所以恳求神农趁早回家。神农摇摇头说："百姓们在挨饿生病，我们怎么能打退堂鼓呢？"

After continuing their trek, they came to the foot of an impassable mountain. All around were cliffs that pierced the clouds. The cliffs were draped with waterfalls and covered with slippery moss. Shen Nong's followers saw no way to go forward unless they had ladders long enough to reach up to heaven. Again, they urged Shen Nong to turn back, but of course he refused. Gazing off into the distance, he suddenly spotted a golden monkey hopping up and down on vines and fallen branches. "Aha!" he thought out loud, "we'll use vines and branches to build ladders up these cliffs!" It took them a full year to build 360 ladders to reach the mountaintop. It is said that modern-day building scaffolds are modeled after Shen Nong's ladders.

Once they reached the top of the mountain, Shen Nong's work began in earnest. While his followers fended off dangerous beasts and built a campsite, Shen Nong went about tasting the exotic plants and observing the effect they had on him. At night, he would sit by a fire and record his findings.

One day Shen Nong tasted something that turned out to be deadly poisonous. But before he lost consciousness, he pointed to a red plant and then to his mouth. His followers understood his gesture and quickly chewed some of the red plant and put it in his mouth. Shen Nong quickly recovered and that is how the wonder drug *linzhicao* was discovered.

Over the course of their journey, Shen Nong discovered 365 medicinal herbs, which are documented in *Shen Nong's Classic of Herbal Medicines*. He also identified the five major grains that became staple foods for the Chinese people.

大家又走了一段，来到一座大山脚下。眼前这座大山挡住了去路，四周都是高耸入云的悬崖峭壁。山崖上挂着一条条瀑布，还长满了青苔。看到眼前的景象，乡民们都觉得除非有通天的云梯，要不然根本上不去。于是大家又劝神农回家吧，神农当然又一次拒绝了。神农注视着前方，突然看见一只金丝猴在树藤和倒了的树干上跳上跳下。神农突然有了主意："对啊，我们就用树藤和树干搭梯子上悬崖！"神农和乡民们花了整整一年的时间，终于搭好了360层的梯子，到达了山顶。据说，现代建房使用的脚手架就来自神农那时候搭建的梯子。

到了山顶以后，神农马上开工了。乡民们一边防备野兽，一边修建营地，而神农则开始尝试奇花异草，观察它们在自己身上的反应。到了晚上，神农就坐在篝火旁边，把自己尝草的心得记录下来。

有一天，神农尝试的一种草毒性很强。在他失去知觉以前，用手指着一种红色的植物，又指了指自己的嘴巴。乡民们明白了他的意思，很快把那种红色植物放到嘴里嚼了嚼，喂给了神农，结果神农被救活了！那种红色的神药因此得名灵芝草。

在这次艰难的行程中，神农一共尝出了365种草药，写成了《神农本草经》。此外，神农也发现了五谷，后来成为了中国人的主食。

With their mission accomplished, the group started their journey down the cliffs. But the ladders they had built had disappeared! Then, lo and behold, they realized that the ladders had taken root and grown into a forest. Just as Shen Nong worried about what to do next, a flock of white cranes lifted him and all his followers and transported them to the palace in heaven.

Postscript

Shen Nong is mentioned in the most ancient historical texts dating back to the fifth century BCE, but only sketchily, because historians purport to record only known facts. In the *Historical Records* by Sima Qian (ca. 100 BCE), it is said that Shen Nong was not an individual but a clan that dominated the region. Eventually this clan declined and was conquered by the clan to which the Yellow Emperor belonged. However, in the Chinese popular consciousness, this grim history of tribal warfare takes a back seat to the colorful myths of Shen Nong, the cultural hero.

Mythmakers did not pretend that Shen Nong was a normal human. He is said to have had a transparent "crystal belly" so that the effect of anything he ingested would be clearly visible. A certain plant would make the heart beat faster, a poisonous one would cause a particular organ to turn black, etc. Alternatively, in some portraits of Shen Nong, he appears as a superhuman semi-beast, perhaps harking back to the golden monkey that inspired the ladders for climbing the cliffs.

神农大功告成以后，一行人就准备下山回家了。但是他们先前搭建的梯子却不见了！哎呀，没想到用来搭建梯子的那些树干早已经生根发芽，长成了一片林海。神农正发愁，不知道怎么办才好，天上飞来了一群白鹤，把神农和乡民们都带到天宫上去了。

后 记

有关神农最早的记载可以追溯到公元前五世纪。不过关于神农的史料只有零星的片言只语，因为历史学家们自称只记录史实。在司马迁（公元前100年）著述的《史记》中，神农并不是一个人，而是当时一个强大的氏族。后来，这个氏族日渐衰落，最后被黄帝所属的氏族征服了。不过，这两个氏族之间的战争史实，在中国民间的意识中，远不如民族英雄神农的传说故事令人印象深刻。

民间传说并没有刻意把神农塑造成一个真人。据说，神农的肚子是透明的，所以他吃进去的东西在消化过程中的反应都能看得一清二楚。某种植物吃下去后会让心脏跳得更快，某种会让某个器官变黑等等。在一些神农的肖像里，他看上去像半人半兽的超人，令人想起给了神农搭建梯子灵感的那只金丝猴。

For those who find the story of Shen Nong being carried to heaven by a white crane too far-fetched, there is an alternative version in which Shen Nong sacrificed his own life to save mankind. After discovering hundreds of medicinal herbs and surviving quite a few close calls, he finally succumbed to a poisonous weed that ruptured his intestines. In another version he was killed after ingesting a centipede. Either way, Shen Nong died as a martyr in service to his people.

Chinese people often express their cultural pride by calling themselves the "descendants of King Yan and King Huang." These two kings are revered as the founding fathers of Chinese civilization. King Huang is known as the Yellow Emperor in the West. As for King Yan, he is none other than the "Divine Agriculturist" Shen Nong.

As the first of two founding fathers of Chinese civilization, Shen Nong was also credited with the invention of farming tools such as the hoe, plow, and ax, as well as well-digging, irrigation, seed storage, the weekly farmers market, the Chinese solar-lunar calendar with the twenty-four seasons, the harvest rite, and even acupuncture and moxibustion. Of course, no Divine Agriculturist or even an entire multigenerational clan could have accomplished all this, but this is a catalog of what the Chinese people believe to be the foundation stones of their agrarian civilization.

Finally, how did the title King Yan become associated with the Divine Agriculturist? The character for Yan (炎) is composed of two fires (火), meaning "flames, burn." So, was King Yan the "Flaming King"? One theory is that Shen Nong also invented slash-and-burn agriculture, a common practice in primitive civilizations.

要是你不愿意相信神农最后被一只白鹤带到了天宫，那么另一个说法是神农为了拯救人类而牺牲了自己的生命。神农尝过几百种草药，有几次差一点被毒死，最终一种叫作断肠草的剧毒植物要了他的命。还有一个说法是神农因为吃了百足虫而死的。无论如何，神农是为了百姓而牺牲了自己生命的民族英雄。

中国人认为炎帝与黄帝是中华文明的缔造者，因此常常自称为"炎黄子孙"。在西方，"黄帝"可以直接翻译成英文，而炎帝实际上就是神农。

作为中华文明两位缔造者之一的神农也发明了农耕的工具和技术，包括锄、犁、斧、挖井灌溉、种子储藏、每周集市、农历二十四节气、腊祭、甚至针灸和艾灸。当然，仅靠一位神农，甚至一整个民族的几代人也无法取得这么伟大的成就，但这一系列的发明，在中国人的心目中代表了祖先农耕文明的基石。

最后，炎帝与神农这两个称谓有什么关系呢？"炎"这个字由两个火组成，意思是"火焰，燃烧"。那么，炎帝就是"燃烧的帝王"吗？据说，神农也发明了刀耕火种，而这也是世界上一种普遍的原始农作方式。

Vocabulary

1. 靠···为生 kào...wéishēng rely on...for livelihood

2. 打猎 dǎliè to hunt

3. 谷物 gǔwù grains

4. 毒草 dúcǎo poisonous weeds

5. 草药 cǎoyào herbs

6. 生后 shēnghòu posthumous

7. 尊称 zūnchēng honorific title; to be honorifically called...

8. 部落首领 bùluò shǒulǐng tribal leader

9. 同情心 tóngqíngxīn sympathetic heart

10. 挨饿 ái'è suffer hunger

11. 遭受 zāoshòu to suffer from

12. 悲伤 bēishāng sorrowful

13. 消灾 xiāozāi to eradicate disasters

14. 祛病 qūbìng to dispel illness

15. 神谕 shényù oracle, divine message

16. 隐居 yǐnjū to live in seclusion

17. 苦思冥想 kǔsī míngxiǎng to wrack one's brains

18. 不为人知 bùwéi rénzhī unknown to people

19. 疗效 liáoxiào healing efficacy

20. 信赖 xìnlài to trust, to depend on

21. 踏上···征程 tàshàng...zhēngchéng to start a journey

22. 水泡 shuǐpào blister

23. 老茧 lǎojiǎn callus

24. 山峰 shānfēng mountain peak

25. 奇花异草 qíhuā yìcǎo strange flowers and grasses

26. 隐约 yǐnyuē indistinct, faint

27. 山谷 shāngǔ valley

28. 窜 cuàn to scurry

29. 豹子 bàozi leopard

30. 蟒蛇 mǎngshé python

31. 挥舞神鞭 huīwǔ shénbiān to wield a magic whip

32. 野兽 yěshòu wild beasts

33. 搏斗 bódòu to fight, to struggle against

34. 条纹 tiáowén stripes

35. 斑点 bāndiǎn spots

36. 伤疤 shāngbā scars

37. 恳求 kěnqiú to beseech, to beg

38. 打退堂鼓 **dǎ tuìtánggǔ** to beat a retreat, to back out

39. 高耸入云 **gāosǒng rùyún** to tower into the clouds

40. 悬崖峭壁 **xuányá qiàobì** hanging cliffs and steep precipices

41. 瀑布 **pùbù** waterfall

42. 青苔 **qīngtái** moss

43. 云梯 **yúntī** tall ladder (lit. cloud ladder)

44. 拒绝 **jùjué** to refuse

45. 注视 **zhùshì** to watch attentively

46. 金丝猴 **jīnsīhóu** golden monkey

47. 搭梯子 **dā tīzi** to build ladders

48. 脚手架 **jiǎoshǒujià** scaffolds

49. 营地 **yíngdì** encampment

50. 篝火 **gōuhuǒ** campfire

51. 心得 **xīndé** what one has learned (lit. mind acquired)

52. 毒性 **dúxìng** poisonous property

53. 知觉 **zhījué** consciousness

54. 嚼 **jiáo** to chew

55. 灵芝草 **língzhīcǎo** a plant with miraculous healing powers

56. 行程 **xíngchéng** journey

57. 主食 **zhǔshí** food staple

58. 生根发芽 **shēnggēn fāyá** to take root and sprout

59. 发愁 **fāchóu** to worry, to fret about

60. 白鹤 **báihè** white crane

61. 天宫 **tiāngōng** palace in heaven

62. 追溯 **zhuīsù** to trace back to

63. 零星 **língxīng** fragmentary

64. 片言只语 **piànyán zhīyǔ** a phrase or two, only a few words

65. 史实 **shǐshí** historical truth

66. 著述 **zhùshù** to write, to compile; written work

67. 氏族 **shìzú** clan

68. 衰落 **shuāiluò** to decline

69. 征服 **zhēngfú** to conquer

70. 民间传说 **mínjiān chuánshuō** folklore, popular legend

71. 刻意 **kèyì** deliberately, intentionally

72. 塑造 **sùzào** to create, to portray

73. 透明 **tòumíng** transparent

74. 消化 **xiāohuà** to digest

75. 心脏 **xīnzàng** heart (organ)

76. 器官 **qìguān** organ

77. 肖像 **xiàoxiàng** portrait

78. 灵感 **línggǎn** inspiration

79. 牺牲 **xīshēng** to sacrifice

80. 断肠草 **duànchángcǎo** poisonous sumac

81. 剧毒 **jùdú** extremely poisonous

82. 百足虫 **bǎizúchóng** centipede

83. 缔造者 **dìzàozhě** creator, founder

84. 炎黄子孙 **Yán Huáng zǐsūn** descendants of emperors Yan and Huang

85. 农耕 **nónggēng** agriculture

86. 锄,犁,斧 **chú, lí, fǔ** hoe, plow, ax

87. 挖井灌溉 **wājǐng guàngài** to dig wells and irrigate

88. 种子储藏 **zhǒngzi chǔcáng** storage of seeds

89. 集市 **jíshì** country market

90. 节气 **jiéqì** the system of 24 seasons in a year

91. 腊祭 **làjì** rituals in the last month of the lunar year

92. 针灸 **zhēnjiǔ** acupuncture

93. 艾灸 **àijiǔ** moxibustion

94. 基石 **jīshí** foundation stone

95. 称谓 **chēngwèi** appellation, title

96. 火焰 **huǒyàn** flame

97. 燃烧 **ránshāo** to burn

98. 刀耕火种 **dāogēng huǒzhòng zhǒng** slash and burn agriculture

Questions for contemplation and discussion

1. Are there some parts of the Shen Nong mythology that remind you of stories from other cultures in the world?

2. In the mythology about Shen Nong, the demarcation between food and medicine is unclear. Can you think of some examples of this in contemporary Chinese cuisine and medicine?

3. Learning to build ladders from observing a monkey is not so far-fetched. Can you think of other important things in human civilization that we have learned from the behavior of animals?

4. From the description of the terrain that Shen Nong and his followers had to negotiate, can you imagine the topography of an actual area in China?

5. There is a debate in the medical field about the efficacy of Western and Eastern medicine as represented mostly by Chinese medicine. What do you think of these two traditions? What do some of your Chinese friends think?

Tamer of the Great Floods

The Great Wall of China is widely recognized as one of the wonders of the ancient world. This story is about a feat of engineering that surpassed the Great Wall by far from the perspective of advancing Chinese civilization, and is almost twice as ancient.

About four thousand years ago, at the dawn of Chinese civilization, the Central Plains of China was ruled by a succession of three sage kings: Yao, Shun, and Yu. At that time Chinese society was loosely organized into tribes, and the supreme ruler was chosen by consensus of the tribal leaders. According to legend, when each of these three kings waned in vitality, he voluntarily yielded his position to a successor deemed worthy by tribal leaders.

In the process of transitioning from a nomadic hunting-gathering society to a settled agrarian society, the greatest adversity facing the ancestors of the Chinese were the frequent devastating floods that not only wiped out their habitats and crops but also decimated the population. Naturally, an important qualification for a ruler was the ability to control the floods and transform them into a resource.

Yao was the first emperor who attempted to bring the floods under control. He convened all the tribal leaders to select a chief engineer for this monumental project. The tribal leaders agreed that Gwen was the best man for the job. Yao disagreed because he knew Gwen was too headstrong for such a complex undertaking, but he went along with the tribal leaders' consensus, as that was the standard practice of the time.

大禹治水

众所周知，长城是中国古代建筑的一大奇迹。然而，从推进中华文明进步的角度来看，这篇故事讲述的水利工程甚至超越了长城，而且比建造长城的时间还早一倍。

大约四千年前，在中华文明的初始时期，中原大地先后由尧、舜、禹三皇统治。那个时候的中国社会是由不同的部落组成的，而最高统治者由部落首领共同选出。根据传说，三皇中的每一位都在年老体衰的时候主动"禅让"，将统治权交给部落首领们认可的继位者。

从依靠狩猎采集为生的社会转变为农耕社会的过程中，人们面对的最大困难就是经常发生的洪涝灾害。大水不但冲毁了人们的家园和庄稼，还夺走了许多人的生命。显然，成为统治者的一个重要条件就是有能力治理水患，并把水力变成一种可用的资源。

第一位试图治理水患的皇帝就是尧。他召集了所有部落的首领，希望选出一位总工程师来完成他的伟业。部落首领们都认为鲧是最合适的人选。不过，尧认为鲧这个人太固执了，承担不了这项复杂的大工程。尽管如此，尧还是按照那个时候的惯例接受了部落首领们提出的人选。

Having received the king's commission, Gwen proceeded to organize each community to build dikes around their village and farmland. The populace supported this approach because they felt their own community was being protected. The dikes needed frequent repairs, and with each flood, they needed to be built higher and wider. After nine years of intensive labor and investment of resources, it became clear that this approach was not going to bring the floods under control.

When Shun succeeded Yao as king, the first thing he did was to personally inspect the flood control projects that Gwen had done. Shocked by what he found, Yao banished Gwen to a remote region. Yao then consulted the tribal leaders to identify a more capable hydro-engineer. To his surprise, they recommended Gwen's son Yu. To

　鲧得到皇帝的<u>任命</u>以后，便开始组织各个社区的百姓在<u>村庄</u>和农田的四周修建<u>大堤</u>。百姓们以为这个方法可以保护自己的社区，所以都很支持鲧的做法。这些大堤需要不断地<u>加固</u>，每次洪涝之后，就变得更高更宽。九年间，百姓为修建大堤<u>耗费</u>了大量的人力物力，但这个方法显然无法治理好水患。

　尧<u>退位</u>以后，舜<u>继承</u>了皇位。他做的第一件事情就是亲自<u>视察</u>鲧治理水患的工程。看到鲧在各处建造的大堤，舜<u>惊呆</u>了，随后将鲧<u>贬</u>到了一个<u>遥远</u>的地方。紧接着，舜<u>征求</u>各部落首领的意见，希望找到一位<u>胜任</u>这项工程的水利工程

Shun's credit, he did not allow Gwen's failure to prejudice him against Yu; to Yu's credit, he did not bear a grudge against Shun for punishing his father.

Yu's approach was radically different from his father's. He knew the project would take years, if not decades, and would require the collaboration of the entire populace. First, he led a team to survey the vast territory impacted by the floods, through all the hills and valleys, even up to the springs that fed the streams that merged into the rivers, and all the way down to where the Yellow River spilled into the sea. This was an extremely arduous journey. Once the team was caught in a massive hurricane, which decimated quite a few and left the survivors terrified. The river near the site of this disaster has since been named "Followers Terrified River" to commemorate the event.

After a complete survey of the terrain, Yu began the monumental task of channeling the huge downpours that frequently but unpredictably devastated the entire region. This involved digging canals, deepening existing streams and rivers, creating reservoirs, connecting the tributaries to the Yellow River, and finally leading the flow out to sea. As the leader, Yu was always the first to start work in the morning and the last to rest. Through his self-sacrifice, he was able to inspire his followers to put forth their best effort.

It took Yu and all the tribes of the region thirteen years to bring the floods under control. Yu then rallied the tribes to harness water resources and promote agriculture, fishery, and animal husbandry. For his accomplishments, Yu was promoted to prime minister under King Shun, and seventeen years later, he succeeded Shun as king by tribal consensus.

师。没想到部落首领们居然推荐了鲧的儿子禹。舜是一位贤明的君主，并没有因为鲧的败绩而歧视禹；禹也是宽厚大度的人，并没有因为舜处罚了自己的父亲而怨恨舜。

禹治理水患的方法与父亲的非常不一样。他知道这项工程不是十年八年就能完成的，而且需要全民合作才能成功。首先，禹带领一队人马，跋山涉水，考察了经常受水患影响的整个地区，从每个支流的发源地一直到黄河的入海口。这是一趟极其艰难的旅程。有一次，他们遭遇了一场罕见的暴风雨，损失了不少人马，剩下的人也被吓坏了。后来，附近的那条河被命名为"徒骇河"，以纪念那次事件。

禹考察完整个地区以后，就启动了这项浩大的工程。他带领大家挖运河、加深河道、修建水库、把黄河的支流与主河道连接起来、以及最终将黄河引入大海。作为总工程师，禹以身作则，总是最早开工，最后收工。看到禹自我献身的精神，大家都深受鼓舞，也都全力以赴地投入了工作。

禹和整个地区所有部落的民众用了整整十三年，终于治好了水患。此后，禹又带领所有的部落利用水资源发展农业、养鱼业和畜牧业。禹因为治理水患有功，被舜帝提升为自己最得力的助手，十七年后，部落首领们一致推选禹继承了舜的皇位。

According to one story, Yu had planned to continue the tradition of passing his reign to a meritorious successor and his personal choice was Boyi, who had been his lifelong right-hand man from the early days of the flood control project. But when he died, the tribal leaders rejected Boyi and chose Yu's eldest son Qi. According to another story, after Yu died, his son Qi defeated Boyi by military force, resulting in the tribal leaders' submission. A third story tells that Yu designated his own son Qi to be his successor. In any case, the ascension of Qi spelled the end of rule by merit and the beginning of rule by dynastic succession. This is how the first dynasty in Chinese history—the Xia—was founded in about 2070 BCE.

Afterword

The Chinese people revere Yu for his achievements that enabled Chinese civilization to survive and advance. But what brought him close to their hearts was his willingness to sacrifice personal yearnings for the sake of public service. As the legend goes, Yu never stepped foot in his own home during the thirteen years that he led the battle against the floods. He had just married when he embarked on the massive project. The first time he passed his home, he heard the cries of his wife in childbirth, but he suppressed the tug at his heart and walked on. The second time, he saw his wife holding their toddler son in her lap, waving to him, but he waved back and walked on. The third time, his ten-year-old son ran and grabbed him by the hand, but Yu just rubbed the boy's head and told him that he would return when the floods had been subdued.

据说，晚年的禹本来打算按照传统将皇位传给一位品行兼优的继位人。在他眼里，伯益是最合适的人选，因为伯益从治理水患之初就一直跟着禹，可以说是他的左膀右臂。但禹去世以后，部落首领们都反对让伯益继位，而是选择了禹的长子启作为新的皇帝。另一个说法是这样的：禹去世以后，儿子启用武力打败了伯益，部落首领们只好同意启成为新皇帝。还有一个说法是禹直接任命了自己儿子启继承皇位。无论如何，启登基成为新皇帝标志着禅让制的结束，开启了朝代世袭制。中国历史上的第一个朝代夏朝就这样在公元前2070年左右建立了。

附 录

中华文明因为大禹治水而得以延续进步，因此中国人都非常敬佩禹，尊称他为大禹。但让中国人更感动的是大禹公而忘私的无我精神。据传说，大禹在治理水患的十三年当中从未踏入家门。大禹刚开启治水的浩大工程时，刚刚成家娶妻。他第一次路过家门口时，听到了妻子生产时的哭泣声，但大禹强忍住自己的感情，痛苦地离开了。第二次路过家门口时，大禹看到妻子抱着他们的小儿子向他招手，他也只向妻儿挥挥手就继续前行了。第三次路过家门口时，十岁的儿子跑过来抓住了爸爸的手，大禹摸摸儿子的头，告诉他水患治好以后爸爸就会回家。

The earliest literary accounts of Yu appeared around 400 BCE, some 1600 years after the purported events, allowing plenty of time for legends and myths to grow around the historical facts. The following tale of how Yu's wife turned into a stone is an example. As this story goes, China was a matrilocal society in ancient times. When Yu began the first phase of the flood control project, the tall, strong, handsome hydro-engineer met the beautiful Nü Jiao at her tribal village, and the two fell in love at first sight. Yu knew that he would have to stay at this village if he married Nü Jiao, so he made the painful choice of giving her up to continue his journey. Yu's absence only made Nü Jiao's heart grow fonder. One day she defied all social mores and went to look for Yu at his work site. The two married and Nü Jiao settled into life at the work camp. Each day, when it came time for lunch break, Yu would sound a drum from where he was working, and Nü Jiao would rush to take lunch to him. One day Yu accidentally tripped a stone, which rolled onto the drum. Nü Jiao quickly grabbed the lunch basket and rushed toward the sound of the drum. But as she was about to reach Yu, he turned into a big, black, menacing bear. She dropped her basket and ran for her life. Yu chased after her, but in his haste forgot to turn himself back into a man. He kept chasing her and she kept fleeing. Before reaching safety, she collapsed from exhaustion and turned into a stone. This story is obviously a myth, but it is also a poignant portrayal of the psychological realities of a wife married to a great man of public service with zero concern for his own family.

有关大禹最早的记载出现在公元前大约400年，相距传说中的大禹治水约1600年。在这么长的一段时间里，有关大禹的故事被增添了许多神话传奇色彩。《禹妻化石》的故事就是一个很好的例子。相传中国的古代是母系社会。大禹刚开启治水大工程的时候，还是个高大健壮、帅气十足的水利工程师。他在一个部落里遇见了女娇，两人一见钟情。大禹知道他要是与女娇成亲就必须留在她的部落里，所以他忍痛放弃了爱情，继续治水大业。而女娇心中对大禹的爱越来越深。终于有一天，女娇不顾社会习俗的礼仪，到工地上找到了大禹，两人就这样把家安在了营地。每到中午吃饭的时间，大禹就在工地上击鼓，女娇听到鼓声就去送饭。有一天，大禹不小心踢到了一块石头，石头滚下山时碰到了鼓。女娇听到了鼓声，急忙前去送饭。女娇快到的时候，看见大禹变成了一头面目狰狞的大黑熊。女娇吓坏了，扔了手中的食物，惊慌地逃跑了。大禹在后面紧追女娇，但急忙中忘了将自己变回人形。她在前面跑，他在后面追。最后女娇精疲力尽，倒在了地上，化作了一块石头。这显然是一个神话故事，不过也刻画了一个舍家为公的伟人之妻辛酸的心理写照。

Vocabulary

1. 众所周知 **zhòng suǒ zhōu zhī** widely known, known to everyone

2. 建筑 **jiànzhù** (architectural) structure; to construct

3. 奇迹 **qíjì** miracle, marvel

4. 推进 **tuījìn** to advance, to push forward

5. 水利工程 **shuǐlì gōngchéng** hydro engineering

6. 超越 **chāoyuè** to surpass

7. 中原 **Zhōngyuán** Central Plains (cradle of Chinese civilization)

8. 尧,舜,禹 **Yáo, Shùn, Yǔ** China's three most ancient legendary kings

9. 统治 **tǒngzhì** to govern

10. 年老体衰 **niánlǎo tǐshuāi** old and physically frail

11. 禅让 **chánràng** to abdicate and yield leadership position

12. 认可 **rènkě** to approve

13. 继位者 **jìwèizhě** successor

14. 狩猎采集 **shòuliè cǎijí** hunting and gathering

15. 洪涝灾害 **hónglào zāihài** flooding as natural disaster

16. 冲毁 **chōnghuǐ** to destroy (by flood)

17. 庄稼 **zhuāngjia** crops

18. 夺走 **duózǒu** to snatch away

19. 治理水患 **zhìlǐ shuǐhuàn** to bring floods under control

20. 资源 **zīyuán** resources

21. 试图 **shìtú** to attempt to...

22. 召集 **zhàojí** to recruit/gather (human resources)

23. 总工程师 **zǒng gōngchéngshī** lead engineer

24. 伟业 **wěiyè** grand project

25. 鲧 **Gǔn** a man's name (Yu's father)

26. 固执 **gùzhí** obstinate

27. 承担 **chéngdān** to undertake, to assume (responsibility)

28. 惯例 **guànlì** precedence

29. 任命 **rènmìng** to appoint

30. 村庄 **cūnzhuāng** village

31. 大堤 **dàdī** big dike

32. 加固 **jiāgù** to strengthen

33. 耗费 **hàofèi** to expend (material and human resources)

34. 退位 **tuìwèi** to retire from a position

35. 继承 **jìchéng** to inherit, to succeed

36. 视察 **shìchá** to inspect

37. 惊呆 **jīngdāi** stunned, shocked

38. 贬 **biǎn** to banish

39. 遥远 **yáoyuǎn** faraway

40. 征求 **zhēngqiú** to seek

41. 胜任 **shèngrèn** competent, qualified (for a certain task)

42. 推荐 **tuījiàn** to recommend

43. 贤明 **xiánmíng** wise

44. 败绩 **bàijì** record of failure

45. 歧视 **qíshì** to discriminate against

46. 宽厚大度 **kuānhòu dàdù** broad-minded

47. 处罚 **chǔfá** to punish

48. 怨恨 **yuànhèn** grudge, enmity

49. 人马 **rénmǎ** troops & forces (not necessarily including horses), capable personnel

50. 跋山涉水 **báshān shèshuǐ** to travel through arduous terrain

51. 考察 **kǎochá** to investigate, to survey

52. 支流 **zhīliú** tributary (of a river)

53. 发源地 **fāyuándì** location of origin

54. 入海口 **rùhǎikǒu** estuary

55. 极其 **jíqí** extremely

56. 旅程 **lǚchéng** journey

57. 遭遇 **zāoyù** to encounter (something dangerous or evil)

58. 罕见 **hǎnjiàn** rare, seldom-seen

59. 损失 **sǔnshī** loss

60. 命名 **mìngmíng** to give a proper name

61. 徒骇河 **Túhàihé** literally "Followers Frightened River"

62. 启动 **qǐdòng** to begin a project

63. 浩大 **hàodà** enormous, grandiose

64. 运河 **yùnhé** canal

65. 水库 **shuǐkù** reservoir

66. 以身作则 **yǐ shēn zuò zé** to use oneself as a model

67. 自我献身 **zìwǒ xiànshēn** to sacrifice oneself

68. 鼓舞 **gǔwǔ** to encourage

69. 全力以赴 **quánlì yǐfù** to give one's all (to a project or cause)

70. 养鱼业 **yǎngyúyè** fish farming

71. 畜牧业 **xùmùyè** animal husbandry

72. 品行兼优 **pǐnxíng jiānyōu** excellent in both morals and actions

73. 左膀右臂 **zuǒbǎng yòubì** right-hand and left-hand man

74. 武力 **wǔlì** military might

75. 无论如何 **wúlùn rúhé** no matter what, in any case

76. 登基 **dēngjī** to ascend to the throne

77. 标志 **biāozhì** to signify, to signal

78. 世袭制 **shìxízhì** hereditary system

79. 延续 **yánxù** to continue, to sustain

80. 敬佩 **jìngpèi** to revere, to esteem

81. 公而忘私 **gōng ér wàngsī** public-minded without regard for oneself

82. 无我精神 **wúwǒ jīngshén** spirit of self-sacrifice

83. 踏入 **tàrù** to embark on

84. 成家娶妻 **chéngjiā qǔqī** (re a man) to take a wife and start a family

85. 哭泣 **kūqì** to weep

86. 强忍住 **qiáng rěnzhù** to bear and suppress (one's emotions)

87. 抓住 **zhuāzhù** to grab onto

88. 相距 **xiāngjù** to be apart by (time or distance)

89. 增添 **zēngtiān** to add

90. 色彩 **sècǎi** colors

91. 母系 **mǔxì** matrilineal

92. 健壮 **jiànzhuàng** physically strong

93. 帅气十足 **shuàiqì shízú** extremely handsome

94. 女娇 **Nǚjiāo** name of a woman

95. 一见钟情 **yījiàn zhōngqíng** love at first sight

96. 成亲 **chéngqīn** to marry

97. 忍痛 **rěntòng** to bear pain

98. 放弃 **fàngqì** to relinquish, to give up

99. 习俗 **xísú** custom

100. 礼仪 **lǐyí** ritual

101. 击鼓 **jīgǔ** to beat a drum

102. 踢 **tī** to kick

103. 滚 **gǔn** to roll

104. 面目狰狞 **miànmù zhēngníng** (re facial features) ferocious

105. 黑熊 **hēixióng** black bear

106. 惊慌 **jīnghuāng** startled, frightened

107. 紧追 **jǐnzhuī** to chase close behind

108. 精疲力尽 **jīngpí lìjìn** totally exhausted

109. 刻画 **kèhuà** to depict, to portray

110. 舍家为公 **shějiā wèigōng** to sacrifice one's family in public service

111. 辛酸 **xīnsuān** heart-wrenching

112. 写照 **xiězhào** portrayal

Questions for contemplation and discussion

1. Can you think of a prehistoric flood story from another culture, or look one up from the Internet? Do you think it has a historical basis like the story of Yu taming the great floods?

2. How was Yu's method of taming the great floods different from his father's? Discuss the differences from both the engineering and administrative perspectives.

3. With Yu's relationship with his wife and family in the background, would you consider marrying someone you love but who is totally dedicated to public service or "married to a career"?

4. What do you think of ancient China's system of "rule by merit"? Why was it replaced by a system of dynastic rule?

5. The Yellow River has been called China's "Mother River" as well as "China's Sorrow." Can you explain why?

The Invention of Chinese Writing

The reign of the Yellow Emperor was a golden age of inventions. With the rise in civilization, governing a society became more complex and the need for record keeping grew enormously. Cang Jie had an amazing memory, so he was appointed by the emperor to keep accounts of domesticated animals and stored food. Eventually, Cang Jie realized that his memory was no longer adequate, so he devised an ingenious system of tying objects to strings. To designate different objects and denominations, he used strings of various colors, different knots, and tokens like shells of different sizes and shapes. This system made Cang Jie's

仓颉造字

黄帝统治时期是发明创造的一个黄金时代。随着文明的兴起，管理一个社会变得更加复杂，对记事的需求大大增加了。仓颉有着惊人的记忆力，所以黄帝让他负责记录圈养的牲畜和存储的食物。后来，仓颉觉得他的脑子也不够用了，就想出了结绳记事的独特方法。他用不同颜色的线，打成不同的结，也用大小不同、形状各异的贝壳来表示不同的东西和单位。这个方法很有效，但并没有减轻仓颉的

job more manageable, but it did not become easier, because the emperor only piled more and more responsibilities on him. Soon he was also tasked with keeping an account of hunting harvests, items used at religious sacrifices, and even births and deaths.

One day, when Cang Jie was part of a hunting expedition, the group came to a crossroads. Three old men argued about which way to go. One said they should go east because that was where they would find antelopes; a second said they should go north because a herd of deer had just gone there; the third said they should go west to hunt down two tigers before they had a chance to attack villagers. Apparently, these three elderly hunters could identify the different footprints left by these animals. "Aha!" Cang Jie thought to himself, "I could use a system of symbols like these footprints to designate different things! This would make my job so much easier!"

When the Yellow Emperor heard rumors about Cang Jie's invention, he immediately dispatched him to all the tribes to teach them the system of symbols for record keeping. This common set of symbols enhanced the emperor's power to govern the various tribes. But as Cang Jie grew in prestige, he became conceited and disrespectful of others, and also a bit lazy and careless in his work. This greatly upset the Yellow Emperor, but he did not punish Cang Jie. Instead, he consulted with a wise old man. "Rest assured, your highness," the old man told the emperor, "I'm sure Cang Jie can be motivated to return to the respectful hardworking man that he used to be."

The old man found Cang Jie in the middle of teaching a group of tribesmen. He quietly sat at the back of the group and listened. Cang Jie's self-pride rose another notch when he saw this dignified old man—with his long beard braided into 120 knots to indicate his age—joining his audience. After the class ended, the old man stayed behind to chat with Cang Jie.

工作量，因为黄帝派给他的活儿越来越多，例如，记录狩猎的收获、祭祀使用的物件，甚至出生和死亡的人数也都由他负责登记了。

有一天，仓颉与几个人一起出门狩猎，来到了一个十字路口。三位老人为了走哪个方向争论起来。一个说东边有羚羊，所以应该往东走；另一个说一群鹿刚往北边去了，所以应该往北走；还有一个说应该往西走，去杀死那边的两只老虎，不然百姓会受到伤害。三位长者显然是从野兽留在地上的足迹看出来的。"对啊！"仓颉恍然大悟道："我可以用一套像这些足迹一样的符号来代表不同的东西啊！这样我的工作更容易了！"

黄帝听到仓颉的新发明以后，马上派他去各个部落，传授用符号系统记事的新方法。这套通用的符号加强了黄帝统治各个部落的力量。不过，随着名望的上升，仓颉变得骄傲自大，目中无人，甚至开始偷懒，工作也不那么认真了。黄帝很不高兴，但并没有惩罚仓颉。黄帝向一位智者请教，智者说："陛下，不用担心，我保证仓颉会恢复原来的样子，尊重别人，勤奋工作的。"

智者找到仓颉的时候，他正在向一群部落百姓传授记事符号。智者静静地坐在他们的后面，认真地听仓颉讲话。这位智者气质不凡，留着长长的胡须，上面打着120个结，表明他120岁了！仓颉看到智者也加入了听众，一下子又骄傲了起来。仓颉讲完后，智者留下来跟他谈了起来。

"I've heard much about your amazing invention, so I decided to come see for myself," said the old man, "Maybe it's my old age, but I had trouble following the logic in some of your symbols. For example, the symbols for horse, donkey, and mule all have four legs, but the one for cow only shows a tail." He continued with more examples of symbols that did not make sense.

Cang Jie realized that the old man was right. What made sense to him did not necessarily make sense to others. He then got down on his knees to thank the old man and apologize for his arrogance and carelessness. The old man held Cang Jie's hands and said, "My son, you've done a wonderful thing for our people. With the writing system that you invented, the knowledge of my generation can now be passed down to later generations. Your name will go down in history! But remember, my son, always be humble, for there is always more to learn from others."

From that day on, Cang Jie analyzed every new symbol more thoroughly. Furthermore, he invited comments and suggestions to make sure the new symbols made sense to everyone before adopting them.

Any narrative of how a writing system came about is inevitably incomplete and murky, but by creating the legend of Cang Jie the Chinese people have found a tangible way to commemorate this awesome cornerstone of their civilization.

"你的发明真了不起，我听到了很多赞美，所以来亲眼见识一下。不过，可能因为我老了，你刚才讲的那些符号当中，有的逻辑我还不太明白。比如，马、驴和骡子的符号都有四条腿，可是牛的符号却只有一条尾巴。"智者接着又说出一些不太合理的符号。

仓颉意识到智者说的话很有道理。可不是嘛，他自己觉得很合理的符号，别人不一定理解。仓颉连忙跪倒在地，为自己的骄傲自大和粗心大意向智者道歉。智者拉起仓颉的手说："孩子，你为大家做了一件大好事。你发明了书写方法，我这一代人的知识就可以世世代代传下去了。你的名字会流芳千古！但是孩子，你要记住，做人要谦虚，别人身上总有可学的东西。"

从那天起，仓颉每造一个符号都很仔细地推敲。此外，他也注意听取别人的意见和建议，得到每个人的认可后才采用这些新的符号。

文字无疑是华夏文明的奠基石。在文字出现以前，任何关于文字形成的历史都不可能是真实完整的。不过，仓颉造字的传说反映了中国人对华夏文明基石的崇敬之情。

Afterword

Civilizations tend to go through periods of cultural growth and innovation. A good example in Chinese history is the Spring and Autumn and Warring States period (ca. 770–221 BCE).[1] This was the era of great classical thinkers and scholars who not only documented their own times but also left an account of the preceding millennia. Not surprisingly, this period of rapid cultural growth coincided with the consolidation of the Chinese writing system, and the two events were mutually enabling.

In 1928 a startling archeological discovery in Anyang (present-day Henan Province) confirmed the existence of the Shang Dynasty (ca. 1600–1046 BCE). The bizarre "oracle bones" found at this site were determined to be the earliest artifacts of a Chinese writing system.[2] These bones—the shoulder blades of oxen and the bottom shells of turtles— had been used by rulers for divination. A question such as "What is an auspicious day for the king to go hunting?" would be posed, a heated poker would be used to generate a crack in the bone, then the answer would be interpreted from the pattern of the crack. The question and answer would then be inscribed on the bone. By the late Shang Dynasty the same writing system appeared on bronzes. Both mediums continued into the early Zhou Dynasty. At the same time, bamboo and wooden slips, as well as woven silk, came into use, and eventually superseded the oracle bones and the bronzes.

---

[1] The name for this period, "Spring and Autumn and Warring States," comes from two historical tracts documenting this period in Chinese history: *Spring and Autumn* by Confucius, and *Record of the Warring States* by Liu Xiang of the Han Dynasty.

[2] Other archeological sites that predate the Anyang site, some as early as 6000 BCE, have yielded pottery shards bearing symbols, but none of them have proven to be a writing system in the sense that they represent sentences.

附 录

在文明发展的历程中往往会出现短暂的大跃进。中国历史上一个典型的例子是春秋战国时代[1]（约公元前770年–公元前221年）。当时涌现了许许多多伟大的思想家和学者，不但记录了他们生活的时代，也留下了关于前几千年的大量记载。这一文化发展中的大跃进与中国文字系统的巩固发生在同一个时期，也可以说两者是相辅相成的。

1928年，震惊中外的河南安阳考古发现证实了商朝（约公元前1600年–公元前1046年）的存在。出土的"甲骨"文物很奇特，后来被证实是中国最早的文字[2]。这些骨头大多是牛肩骨和海龟底壳，被当时的统治者用来占卜。比如，"适合君王出行狩猎的吉日是哪一天？"这样的问题提出来以后，用一支烧热的拨火棍在骨头上灼出一个裂缝，再根据裂缝的形状来解答问题。问题和答案随后都刻在骨头上。到了商朝末期，同样的文字出现在了青铜上。甲骨和青铜一直使用到周朝。与此同时，竹简和木条，以及绢丝也用作了书写材料，最终取代了甲骨和青铜。

---

[1] "春秋战国"的名称取自中国历史上记录那个时期的两部著述，一部是孔子的《春秋》，另一部是汉朝刘向的《战国策》。

[2] 安阳之前的一些考古遗址，有的早在公元前6000年，挖掘出了一些带有符号的陶器碎片，但都没有证实那些符号是可以组成句子的文字系统。

The writing system found on the oracle bones was quite sophisticated. In fact, it had all the principles of character formation present in China's modern writing system. We can surmise that oracle bone writing had evolved from much earlier antecedents. Archeology elsewhere in the world has revealed other writing systems that predate China's oracle bones, most notably the Sumerian cuneiform (ca. 3500 BCE–75 CE). Interestingly, the Sumerian system also began as a logographic system, but it evolved into a hybrid semanto-phonetic system, making it possible to reduce the number of graphs from about one thousand in older texts to four hundred in later texts. In contrast, the Chinese system has changed little since the days of oracle bones, so one still needs to learn about three thousand characters to be fully literate. Most other written languages of the world, with the major exception of Japanese, have adopted phonetic systems. Has China fallen behind the rest of the world in this regard?

The Chinese people do not lack inventiveness. They have in fact devised numerous phonetic systems, but by conscious choice have retained the logographic system for its many advantages. The most outstanding advantage is its ability to accommodate China's vast dialectal diversity, thereby playing an essential role in keeping China unified.

In the early days of the computer revolution, many people felt that computer processing of the Chinese writing system would be an insurmountable challenge. But within a short time several systems of Chinese word processing were developed, some based on phonetics, others on character formation. Today the most widely used system is based on the *pinyin* system, but due to the large number of homophones in Chinese, a process of disambiguation is needed to achieve accuracy. The system that has proven to be the best in terms of speed and accuracy is one based on character formation. Ironically, this system is named "Cang Jie" in honor of the legendary creator of Chinese writing.

商朝时期的甲骨文相当复杂巧妙，已经具有了中国现代汉字构成的所有规则。我们可以推测甲骨文是从更早期的书写方法演变而来的。然而，世界其他地区曾出土过比中国甲骨文更早的书写系统，其中最著名的是苏美尔楔形文字(约公元前3500年－公元75年)。有趣的是，苏美尔楔形文字也起源于一种表意文字，后来才慢慢地演变为意音混合的文字系统，从而能够将古文字系统中大约1000个字符减少到后期的400个左右。不同的是，中文文字从甲骨文以来变化不大，成人必须掌握大约3000个字才算是达到了识字水平。除了日文以外，世界上大多数的书面语言都采用了语音系统。难道中国在这方面比世界其他地区落后吗？

　　中国人并不缺乏创新精神。实际上，他们发明过很多种语音系统，但还是坚持保留了表意文字。这当然是因为表意文字有很多优点，最突出的一个就是能够兼顾中国众多的方言，从而在保持中国统一的方面起到了关键的作用。

　　计算机革命发生的初期，很多人认为计算机处理汉字是一个难以克服的挑战。然而没过多久，专家们就发明了好几种汉字处理系统，有的基于语音，也有的基于汉字构成。今天，使用最广的汉字处理软件基于拼音系统。不过，由于汉语有大量的同音字，打出字以后往往还需要经过挑选。目前，在速度和准确度两方面都最理想的系统是一种基于字形构成的软件。有趣的是，这个系统被命名为"仓颉"，以纪念创造汉字的传奇人物。

Vocabulary

1. 兴起 **xīngqǐ** to rise, to spring up
2. 惊人 **jīngrén** amazing
3. 圈养 **quānyǎng** to raise in pens
4. 牲畜 **shēngxù** livestock
5. 存储 **cúnchǔ** to store
6. 结绳记事 **jiéshéng jìshì** to record by knotting strings
7. 结 **jié** knot
8. 形状各异 **xíngzhuàng gèyì** various different shapes
9. 贝壳 **bèiké** shell
10. 狩猎 **shòuliè** to hunt
11. 祭祀 **jìsì** to offer sacrifices (to gods or ancestors)
12. 登记 **dēngjì** to register
13. 争论 **zhēnglùn** to debate
14. 羚羊 **língyáng** antelope
15. 鹿 **lù** deer
16. 伤害 **shānghài** to harm
17. 长者 **zhǎngzhě** elders
18. 野兽 **yěshòu** beast
19. 足迹 **zújì** footprint
20. 恍然大悟 **huǎngrán dàwù** to suddenly realize
21. 符号 **fúhào** symbol
22. 部落 **bùluò** tribe
23. 传授 **chuánshòu** to transmit (knowledge), to teach
24. 名望 **míngwàng** fame
25. 骄傲自大 **jiāo'ào zìdà** proud and arrogant
26. 目中无人 **mùzhōng wúrén** to look down on everyone
27. 惩罚 **chéngfá** to punish
28. 智者 **zhìzhě** wise man
29. 陛下 **bìxià** Your Majesty
30. 恢复 **huīfù** to recover
31. 勤奋 **qínfèn** diligent
32. 气质不凡 **qìzhì bùfán** impressive appearance
33. 胡须 **húxū** beard
34. 赞美 **zànměi** to praise
35. 见识 **jiànshi** to see and experience
36. 逻辑 **luójí** logic
37. 驴 **lú** donkey
38. 骡子 **luózi** mule
39. 尾巴 **wěibā** tail
40. 意识到 **yìshídào** to realize

41. 连忙 **liánmáng** quickly

42. 跪倒 **guìdǎo** to kneel

43. 粗心大意 **cūxīn dàyì** careless, haphazard

44. 道歉 **dàoqiàn** to apologize

45. 世世代代 **shìshì dàidài** through many generations

46. 流芳千古 **liúfāng qiāngǔ** famous through the ages

47. 谦虚 **qiānxū** modest, self-effacing

48. 仔细 **zǐxì** meticulous

49. 推敲 **tuīqiāo** to analyze, to deliberate

50. 听取 **tīngqǔ** to listen to

51. 认可 **rènkě** to approve

52. 无疑 **wúyí** undoubtedly

53. 奠基石 **diànjīshí** cornerstone

54. 任何 **rènhé** any

55. 形成 **xíngchéng** to form

56. 反映 **fǎnyìng** to reflect

57. 华夏 **Huáxià** a historical word for China

58. 崇敬 **chóngjìng** to respect, to revere

59. 历程 **lìchéng** process, course

60. 短暂 **duǎnzàn** short

61. 大跃进 **dàyuèjìn** Great Leap Forward

62. 典型 **diǎnxíng** typical, classic

63. 春秋战国 **Chūnqiū Zhànguó** Spring and Autumn and Warring States (a period in ancient China)

64. 涌现 **yǒngxiàn** to emerge, to surface

65. 巩固 **gǒnggù** to consolidate

66. 相辅相成 **xiāngfǔ xiāngchéng** mutually enabling

67. 震惊 **zhènjīng** to shock, to startle

68. 考古 **kǎogǔ** archeology

69. 证实 **zhèngshí** to confirm

70. 出土 **chūtǔ** to unearth (lit. to come out of the soil)

71. 甲骨 **jiǎgǔ** oracle bones

72. 文物 **wénwù** cultural artifacts

73. 牛肩骨 **niújiāngǔ** ox shoulder bone

74. 海龟底壳 **hǎiguī dǐké** turtle bottom shell

75. 占卜 **zhānbǔ** divination

76. 吉日 **jírì** auspicious day

77. 拨火棍 **bōhuǒgùn** poker (used in a fire)

78. 灼 **zhuó** to burn

79. 裂缝 **lièfèng** crack

80. 刻 **kè** to carve

81. 青铜 **qīngtóng** bronze

82. 与此同时 **yǔcǐ tóngshí** at the same time

83. 竹简 **zhújiǎn** bamboo slips

84. 绢丝 **juànsī** silk

85. 取代 **qǔdài** to replace

86. 巧妙 **qiǎomiào** ingenious

87. 构成 **gòuchéng** to constitute, to form

88. 规则 **guīzé** rules and regulations

89. 推测 **tuīcè** to deduce

90. 演变 **yǎnbiàn** to evolve; evolution

91. 苏美尔楔形文字 **Sūměi'ěr xiēxíng wénzì** Sumerian cuneiform

92. 起源 **qǐyuán** origin

93. 表意文字 **biǎoyì wénzì** ideogram, script that expresses meaning

94. 意音混合 **yìyīn hùnhé** combination of meaning and sound

95. 从而 **cóngér** thereby

96. 字符 **zìfú** character, symbol

97. 掌握 **zhǎngwò** to master, to grasp

98. 采用 **cǎiyòng** to adopt, to use

99. 语音系统 **yǔyīn xìtǒng** phonetic system

100. 落后 **luòhòu** backward

101. 缺乏 **quēfá** to lack

102. 创新精神 **chuàngxīn jīngshén** innovative spirit

103. 坚持 **jiānchí** to persist in

104. 优点 **yōudiǎn** advantage

105. 突出 **tūchū** to stand out; outstanding

106. 兼顾 **jiāngù** to accommodate (two or more factors)

107. 众多 **zhòngduō** numerous

108. 关键 **guānjiàn** essential, crucial

109. 计算机革命 **jìsuànjī gémìng** computer revolution

110. 处理 **chǔlǐ** to deal with

111. 难以 **nányǐ** difficult to...

112. 克服 **kèfú** to overcome

113. 基于 **jīyú** on the basis of...

114. 软件 **ruǎnjiàn** software

115. 挑选 **tiāoxuǎn** to select

116. 速度 **sùdù** speed

117. 准确度 **zhǔnquèdù** accuracy

118. 命名 **mìngmíng** to give the name

119. 传奇 **chuánqí** legend

fn. 挖掘 **wājué** to dig up

Questions for contemplation and discussion

1. What are the positive and negative traits of Cang Jie's personality? What do you think of the way the Yellow Emperor and the wise old man interacted with him?

2. If you have learned 1,000 or more characters, you must have worked hard to reach this point. Congratulations! Have you noticed any patterns in how characters are formed? Have these patterns helped you remember the characters?

3. How would you compare the current Chinese writing system to a phonetic system? Would you be in favor of China adopting a phonetic system?

4. Now that computer processing of Chinese writing has displaced handwriting, is there any value in learning to write Chinese by hand? Explain your answer.

5. If you have Chinese friends who hail from mainland China, Hong Kong, and Taiwan, do they all speak standard Mandarin? If not, ask them what character input system they prefer and why.

How Silk Was Invented

The Yellow Emperor is revered by the Chinese people as the founding father of their civilization, chiefly because his reign was a golden age of inventions. His own favorite invention was undoubtedly silk making, for he in fact married the inventor Leizu.[1]

Leizu came from a humble family in the Xiling tribe. Like all girls in her tribe, she contributed to her family's livelihood from a young age. One of her jobs was foraging for edible nuts and berries. Apart from being hardworking, Leizu was exceptionally intelligent and compassionate. In those days clothing was made from tree bark and leaves, plus some ragged animal skins and furs. These were not only unsightly but often there were not enough materials to go around. Leizu felt there must be a better way to make clothing.

One day, while foraging in the wild, Leizu found a tree laden with berries. Some had already ripened but others were still green. As she started picking the berries, she noticed a swarm of caterpillar-like worms nibbling at some leaves. Some larger ones were standing still, wiggling their heads back and forth, spitting thread out of their mouths. She quickly filled her basket with berries but made a mental note to return for more later. When she returned a few days later, the "caterpillars" were gone, but attached to the branches nearby were some egg-colored nut-shaped objects. They looked edible, but to be safe Leizu

---

[1] The beginning of the Yellow Emperor's reign in 2698 BCE is reckoned to be the official founding of Chinese civilization. Thus, the year 2024 of the Gregorian calendar is the year 4722 of the Yellow Emperor calendar. The meaning of the name Leizu 嫘祖 is significant. The character 祖 means "ancestor." 嫘 is made up of three components. The component 田 (archaic 畾) indicates the pronunciation of the character. The other two hint at the person: 女 indicates "female" while 糸 (archaic form 帚) is a pictograph of two cocoons linked by silk threads.

丝绸女神嫘祖

黄帝统治中华大地的时期是发明创造的一个黄金时代，黄帝因而被尊为中华文明的始祖。黄帝最欣赏的发明就是丝绸，甚至还娶了丝绸女神嫘祖为妻[1]。

嫘祖出生在西陵部落的一个普通家庭里。她跟部落里的其他女孩子一样，从小就得为全家人的生计干活儿，包括去野外摘可以吃的果子。嫘祖不但很勤劳，也特别聪明，还很有爱心。那个时候，大家穿的都是树皮和树叶，再加上一些破烂的动物皮毛，实在很难看，还常常供不应求。嫘祖看在眼里，心想大家都应该穿得更好啊。

有一天，嫘祖到野外去找吃的，发现一棵树上结满了果子，有的已经熟透了，有的还是青的。她开始摘果子的时候，看见一群毛毛虫一样的虫子在啃树叶，有些大一点的呆着不动，头来回摆动，口吐着线。嫘祖很快摘满了一篮子果子，心里记住了这个地方，想过几天再回来。过了几天，嫘祖回来的时候，发现那些毛毛虫不见了，但旁边的树枝上有一些像坚果一样的蛋黄色的东西，看起来可以吃，但嫘祖觉得应该小心一点，还是先带回家煮一煮。那天，嫘祖摘了半篮子果子，另一半装了蛋黄色的神秘"坚果"。她把"坚果"放

---

[1] 黄帝统治始于公元前2698年，也被认定为中华文明的元年。因此，公历2024年就是黄历4722年。嫘祖这个名字的意思很重要。祖就是"祖先"的祖，而"嫘"字是由三个部分组成的。田（古字畾）代表嫘的音符，另外两个部分暗指人：女表明女性，而糸（古字宗）是象形文字，意思是丝线连接的两个茧。

decided to boil them first. That day Leizu filled half her basket with berries and the other half with the mystery "nuts." When she put the "nuts" in a pot and brought them to a boil, she was amazed to see filaments unravelling from the "nuts." From that surprising discovery, Leizu went on to develop silk yarn and cloth, which turned out to be finer and softer than anything made from plant fibers. With further experimentation, she found this cloth to be superior to all other materials for clothing although it took a lot more work to produce a garment.

Within a short time Leizu passed on her invention by teaching it to others in the tribe. The Xiling chieftain was so delighted with her that he adopted her as his own daughter. Eventually, she was nominated to be the chieftain, but another event intervened.

After news of Leizu and her invention had travelled far and wide, countless ambitious young men from other tribes came to propose marriage but Leizu was not impressed with any of them. Finally, the

进一个锅里，煮开了之后，惊讶地发现细丝从"坚果"上散开来了。有了这个惊人的发现之后，嫘祖纺出了丝纱，也织出了丝绸布料，比其他植物纤维织出的布料都更细腻柔软。做过更多的尝试之后，嫘祖发现用丝绸做衣服比其他布料舒服得多，但也得费更大的功夫。

没过多久，嫘祖就开始在部落里教大家怎么纺织丝绸了。西陵首领非常高兴，就把嫘祖收养为自己的女儿。后来，嫘祖被提名为西陵首领，不过这时候发生了另一件事情。

嫘祖发明丝绸的消息很快就传开了，其他部落的有为青年纷纷前来提亲，但嫘祖一个都没看上。后来，轩辕部落的

young tribal leader from Xuanyuan, on his campaign to unite other tribes, arrived in Xiling. What began as mutual admiration between the two soon blossomed into love. Their marriage also brought about the first peaceful union between two tribes.

When Leizu arrived at Xuanyuan with her husband, the first thing she asked him to do was plant a grove of mulberry trees, for she wanted to continue improving her invention. She domesticated the silkworm and genetically modified the mulberry tree, making both more suitable for silk production. She also invented a reel for joining multiple silk filaments into a thread and adapted the loom to work specifically with silk.

In due course, the Xuanyuan chieftain united all the other tribes and became the Yellow Emperor. He and his wife Leizu devoted the rest of their lives to the advancement of Chinese civilization. Leizu's most notable accomplishment was inculcating a code of morality among the people, including devotion between spouses, loving care for the young, respect for the elderly, and kindness to all others. Under the leadership of the Yellow Emperor and Leizu, society became harmonious and prosperous.

Afterword

The earliest historical record of Leizu, written by the Han Dynasty historian Sima Qian (145–86 BCE), was not nearly as colorful as the above story. It was brief and to the point, and in fact did not even mention the invention of silk: "The Yellow Emperor lived in the hills of Xuanyuan. He married a girl named Leizu from the Xiling clan. She became his official wife and bore him two sons. Later, he dominated 'all under heaven.'"

Yet Leizu has become a very popular figure in Chinese folklore. Our story here of Leizu is only one of many. There are also at least ten locations in present-day China that claim to be her home, Xiling.

年轻首领为了统一其他部落来到了西陵。两人的感情从相互欣赏很快就进入了相亲相爱。不久后，两人结为了夫妻，开启了部落之间和平统一的先河。

嫘祖随丈夫来到轩辕后，希望继续改进丝绸生产，因此让丈夫做的第一件事就是栽种了一片桑树。她把野生的蚕变成了家养蚕，也对桑树做了基因改造，使两者更有利于丝绸生产。她还发明了一种卷轴，可以把很多根细丝合并成一根线；并改造了织布机，专门用来纺织丝绸。

随后，轩辕首领统一了其他部落，成为了黄帝。他和妻子嫘祖共同为中华文明的进步奉献了一生。嫘祖最显著的成就就是教育民众遵循一种道德准则，包括夫妻恩爱、尊老爱幼和善待他人。在黄帝和嫘祖的领导下，社会一片和谐繁荣的景象。

附录

有关嫘祖最早的历史记载出自汉代历史学家司马迁（公元前145年－公元前86年）。他笔下记录的嫘祖远没有前面的故事那么丰富多彩，简短的几句话里甚至都没有提到丝绸的发明："黄帝居轩辕之丘，娶西陵氏之女，是为嫘祖。嫘祖为黄帝正妃，生二子，其后皆有天下。"

然而，嫘祖却成为了中国民间传说中最受欢迎的人物。有关嫘祖的故事数不胜数，这里写的只是其中之一。在今天的中国，至少有十个地方声称是嫘祖的故乡西陵。

Folklore aside, since the early twentieth century archeology has yielded a great deal of information about the history of silk. Amazingly, silk was already in use in the Neolithic Yangshao culture in 4000–3000 BCE. This predated the era of Leizu by one millennium, so the real pioneers of silk production might have been some distant ancestors of hers.

The earliest evidence of silk production, found at a Yangshao culture site in present-day Shanxi Province, was a cocoon cut in half with a sharp knife. Scientists have determined that this cocoon came from a domesticated species. At another Yangshao culture site in present-day Zhejiang Province, fragments of a cloth-making device were found. However, by far the most exciting archeological evidence of silk was a cloth swaddling an infant for burial, dating from around 3630 BCE, found at a site in Henan Province.

The use of silk cloth as a material on which to write and paint was well underway by the Warring States period (ca. 475–221 BCE).[2] In 1942 a fairly well-preserved silk manuscript containing calligraphy and painting from the ancient state of Chu was found in an archeological site in Changsha, Hunan Province.[3] To date, no earlier predecessors of this artifact have been found, but the sophistication in the calligraphy and painting suggests a long process of prior development.

Until recent times silk was a luxury reserved for royalty and the upper class. There were always more affordable alternatives to silk. For writing, the more common bamboo and wooden slips co-existed with silk cloth until they were superseded by paper in second century CE during the late Han Dynasty. During the Tang Dynasty, the color of silk garments was an indicator of social class. The luxury status of silk also made it the preeminent trade commodity between China and the West,

---

[2] See footnote 1 on p. 58.

[3] This site did not become an archeological site until 1973 when it was excavated by Chinese archeologists from the Hunan Museum. However, it had been earlier discovered by tomb robbers in 1942. Among the items stolen was the piece of silk bearing calligraphy and painting, which found its way to the United States and is currently housed at the Freer Sackler Gallery in Washington DC. Dispute over its proprietorship has yet to be resolved.

传说归传说，二十世纪初以来的考古研究发现了大量有关丝绸历史的资料。令人惊讶的是，在公元前4000年－公元前3000年新石器时代的仰韶文化中丝绸就已经出现了，比嫘祖还早一千年。因此，丝绸的发明者可能还是嫘祖的祖先呢！

丝绸生产最早的出土文物是在今天山西省的一处仰韶文化遗址发现的，一把锋利的刀将一个蚕茧切成了两半。科学家确定这是家养蚕结的茧。在今天浙江省的另一处仰韶文化遗址发现了一台原始织布机的碎片。至今最令人激动的出土文物是在河南省的一处考古遗址发现的，一块用来包裹婴儿尸体的丝绸布料，时间可以追溯到大约公元前3630年。

到了战国时期(约公元前475年－公元前221年)[2]，丝绸已经广泛地用于书写和绘画了。1942年，在湖南长沙的考古遗址发现了一幅保存较好的楚国字画[3]。这是至今最古老的一幅字画文物，而其高超的艺术表明已经历了一段漫长的发展。

直到近代，丝绸一直是皇室和上层社会的专用奢侈品。在一般情况下，人们总是有比丝绸简朴的材料可用。比如，在汉朝末期(公元二世纪)纸张普及之前，最通用的书写材料是竹简和木条。在唐朝，丝绸服装的颜色代表着上层社会不同的等级。在中国与西方的贸易史中，丝绸早在汉朝已成为

---

[2] 见58页"仓颉造字"注一。

[3] 实际上，中国湖南省博物馆的考古学家们直到1973年才开始发掘这个遗址。但是，盗墓者在1942年就偷盗了遗址的墓穴。在被盗的物品中有一幅丝绸字画，后被运送到了美国，目前收藏在华盛顿特区的弗里尔塞克勒画廊。这件物品的所有权至今仍存在争议。

and that in turn spurred the emergence of the Silk Road between China and the Mediterranean during the height of the Roman Empire.

To return to Leizu's first intuition that the cocoons she found in the wild were edible, as it turns out, she was right! In the process of silk production, nothing is wasted. To this day in China and other Asian countries, silkworm pupae, a byproduct of sericulture, are a delicacy, highly prized for their taste, nutrition, and even medicinal value.

Vocabulary

1. 丝绸 **sīchóu** silk

2. 始祖 **shǐzǔ** original ancestor, progenitor

3. 欣赏 **xīnshǎng** to appreciate

4. 部落 **bùluò** tribe

5. 生计 **shēngjì** livelihood

6. 摘 **zhāi** to pick

7. 勤劳 **qínláo** diligent

8. 破烂 **pòlàn** tattered

9. 皮毛 **pímáo** skin and fur

10. 供不应求 **gōng búyìng qiú** supply insufficient to meet demand

11. 熟透 **shútòu** fully ripened

12. 青 **qīng** green

13. 毛毛虫 **máomaochóng** caterpillar

14. 啃 **kěn** to gnaw, to nibble

15. 摆动 **bǎidòng** to swing back and forth

16. 吐 **tǔ** to spit out

17. 坚果 **jiānguǒ** nut

18. 煮 **zhǔ** to boil, to cook

19. 神秘 **shénmì** mysterious

20. 锅 **guō** cooking pot

21. 惊讶 **jīngyà** to be surprised

22. 散开 **sànkāi** to spread out, to unravel

23. 纺 **fǎng** to spin

24. 丝纱 **sīshā** silk yarn

了最重要的奢侈商品，由长安一直通到地中海的丝绸之路也因此在罗马帝国的鼎盛时期形成了。

回到嫘祖在野外发现蚕茧时候的情景，直觉告诉她这东西是可以吃的。没错！在丝绸生产的过程中，任何副产品都没有浪费，缫丝后留下的蚕蛹是可以吃的，而且味道独特，富有营养和药用价值。在中国和亚洲其他国家，蚕蛹一直是人们喜爱的一道美味佳肴。

25. 织 **zhī** to weave

26. 植物纤维 **zhíwù xiānwéi** plant fibers

27. 细腻柔软 **xìnì róuruǎn** delicate and soft

28. 尝试 **chángshì** to try (to do something)

29. 提名 **tímíng** to nominate

30. 有为 **yǒuwéi** accomplished

31. 纷纷 **fēnfēn** one after another

32. 提亲 **tíqīn** to propose marriage

33. 夫妻 **fūqī** husband and wife

34. 开启 **kāiqǐ** to open up, to begin

35. 先河 **xiānhé** first of its kind

36. 栽种 **zāizhòng** to plant

37. 桑树 **sāngshù** mulberry tree

38. 蚕 **cán** silkworm

39. 基因 **jīyīn** gene

40. 有利于 **yǒulì yú** beneficial to

41. 卷轴 **juànzhóu** reel

42. 织布机 **zhībùjī** loom (lit. weave cloth machine)

43. 奉献 **fèngxiàn** to dedicate oneself (to common good)

44. 显著 **xiǎnzhù** notable, outstanding

45. 遵循 **zūnxún** to follow (customs, rules, etc.)

46. 准则 **zhǔnzé** guideline

47. 恩爱 **ēn'ài** loving

48. 尊老爱幼 **zūnlǎo àiyòu** to respect the old and love the young

49. 善待 **shàndài** to treat with kindness

50. 和谐繁荣 **héxié fánróng** harmonious and prosperous

51. 景象 **jǐngxiàng** scenario

52. 记载 **jìzǎi** to record

53. 丰富多彩 **fēngfù duōcǎi** rich and colorful

54. 数不胜数 **shǔ búshèng shǔ** countless

55. 声称 **shēngchēng** to claim (fame)

56. 故乡 **gùxiāng** original home

57. 考古 **kǎogǔ** archeology

58. 资料 **zīliào** material

59. 新石器时代 **xīn shíqì shídài** neolithic era

60. 仰韶文化 **Yǎngsháo wénhuà** Yangshao Culture (neolithic Henan site)

61. 出土文物 **chūtǔ wénwù** unearthed cultural relics

62. 遗址 **yízhǐ** ruins, ancient or former site

63. 锋利 **fēnglì** sharp (blade)

64. 蚕茧 **cánjiǎn** silkworm cocoon

65. 原始 **yuánshǐ** primitive, original

66. 碎片 **suìpiàn** fragments

67. 激动 **jīdòng** excited

68. 包裹 **bāoguǒ** to wrap; package

69. 尸体 **shītǐ** corpse

70. 追溯 **zhuīsù** to trace back

71. 广泛 **guǎngfàn** widely

72. 绘画 **huìhuà** painting

73. 楚国 **Chǔguó** State of Chu

74. 高超 **gāochāo** superior

75. 皇室 **huángshì** royal family

76. 奢侈品 **shēchǐpǐn** luxury goods

77. 简朴 **jiǎnpǔ** simple, plain

78. 普及 **pǔjí** to become common

79. 竹简 **zhújiǎn** bamboo slips

80. 木条 **mùtiáo** wooden strips

81. 等级 **děngjí** grade, class

82. 贸易 **màoyì** trade

83. 地中海 **Dìzhōnghǎi** Mediterranean Sea

84. 鼎盛 **dǐngshèng** heyday, at its height

85. 情景 **qíngjǐng** scene, situation

86. 副产品 **fùchǎnpǐn** byproduct

87. 缫丝 **sāosī** to reel silk floss (from silkworm cocoons)

88. 蚕蛹 **cányǒng** silkworm chrysalis

89. 营养 **yíngyǎng** nutrition

90. 美味佳肴 **měiwèi jiāyáo** culinary delicacy

fn1. 元年 **yuánnián** the first year

fn2. 音符 **yīnfú** phonetic symbol

fn3. 象形文字 **xiàngxíng wénzì** pictographic script

fn4. 发掘 **fājué** to excavate

fn5. 盗墓者 **dàomùzhě** grave robbers

fn6. 墓穴 **mùxué** grave pit, open grave

fn7. 收藏 **shōucáng** to collect

fn8. 所有权 **suǒyǒuquán** proprietorship

fn9. 争议 **zhēngyì** controversy

Questions for contemplation and discussion

1. Why is there such a big difference between Sima Qian's succinct historical account of Leizu and the elaborate folklore about her?

2. What are the ideals of womanhood characterized by Leizu in this story? Does this characterization match the traditional Chinese view of womanhood as you understand it?

3. In your opinion, what role does archeology have in substantiating or disproving legends?

4. What is the significance of the Silk Road in world history? Does it have anything in common with China's twenty-first century Belt and Road initiative?

5. The invention of silk originated from an accidental discovery. Can you think of some other examples of this phenomenon in human history?

Lu Ban the Master Craftsman and Builder

The name Lu Ban is enshrined in the two most prestigious prizes in China's construction industry today: the Lu Ban Prize for Excellent Construction Projects, and the Lu Ban Cup for Graduation Projects in BIM Design.[1] Lu Ban, a master craftsman and builder from over 2,400 years ago, has been a household name throughout Chinese history and is, in fact, revered by builders as their patron god. One sign of this deification is the myth that Lu Ban invented virtually all the basic tools of carpentry.

Mythology aside, the stories of Lu Ban's inventions exhibit some exceptional personality traits cherished by the Chinese people. One of these traits—the ability to turn an adversity into a surprising achievement—is illustrated by how two of Lu Ban's inventions came about.

Lu Ban was commissioned by the king of Lu to build a new palace, for which extra-large tree trunks were needed. The standard tool for felling trees in those days was just the ax. Lu Ban had the most skillful workmen under his command but meeting the king's deadline still seemed an impossible task. One day, while taking a shortcut up the hill, Lu Ban slipped and grabbed a clump of tall grass to break his fall. Soon he noticed blood from a gash on his palm. How could an ordinary blade of grass cause such a gash? He then broke off a blade of the same grass and looked at it more closely. That is when he noticed that both edges were serrated. When he lightly drew one serrated edge across the back of his hand, sure enough, it made a cut! The next thing

---

[1] Cf. Website: What Is BIM | Building Information Modeling | Autodesk

鲁班的传说

在今天的中国，建筑行业最负盛名的两项大奖都冠以了鲁班的名字：中国建设工程鲁班奖和鲁班杯BIM设计毕业作品[1]。作为2400多年前的工匠与建筑大师，鲁班的名字在中国历史上的各个朝代都家喻户晓，而他也是业内人士崇拜的祖师爷。根据神话传说，木匠们使用的基本工具几乎都是由鲁班发明的。

神话归神话，鲁班在创造发明的过程中确实体现了一些中国人珍视的非凡性格特征，其中之一就是变害为利，不经意间就取得了开创性的成就。这一特点可由下面的两则故事来证实。

鲁班受鲁王之命建造一座新的宫殿，于是需要一些特大的树干。那时候，砍伐树木的工具就是普通的斧头。鲁班手下有最熟练的工匠，但看起来也无法在鲁王规定的期限内完工。有一天，鲁班走近道上山，脚下一滑，他赶紧一把抓住了身旁的野草才没有滑倒。很快，他注意到手掌上划了一道流着血的口子。鲁班心想，一根普通的野草怎么划了那么大的一个口子呢？随后，他又摘了一棵同样的草，仔细看了看。原来这种草的叶片两边都是锯齿状的。鲁班用这根野草在手背上轻轻一划，果然又划了一道口

---

[1] Cf. Website: What Is BIM | Building Information Modeling | Autodesk

he noticed was a large locust gnawing hungrily on some tough weeds. Taking a closer look at the locust, he saw that it too had a serrated edge across its mandibles. These two discoveries inspired Lu Ban to create a saw blade with a serrated edge. This invention increased the workmen's efficiency enormously, and they were able to complete the new palace ahead of schedule.

Soon Lu Ban's fame spread far and wide, bringing with it the jealousy of a rival by the name of Wen Gong. Both were commissioned by the king to renovate a palace. In an attempt to sabotage Lu Ban's work, Wen Gong surreptitiously cut a couple of inches off Lu Ban's carpentry ruler. This dastardly act was not discovered until Lu Ban's crew had finished cutting all the pillars. By the time Lu Ban realized that the pillars were too short, all the timber had been used up. In a flash, Lu Ban came up with the idea of placing the pillars on top of stone blocks. This

子！接着，他看见一只大蝗虫在飞快地啃着一种看上去很坚挺的野草。凑近一看，鲁班发现这只蝗虫的下颚也是锯齿状的。这两个发现一下子给了鲁班灵感，他随后就发明了一边是锯齿形的锯片。这项新发明大大提高了工匠们的效率，新的宫殿也提前完工了。

鲁班很快就远近闻名了。不过，这也招来了竞争对手文公的嫉妒。鲁班与文公都受鲁王之命，整修一座宫殿。为了陷害鲁班，文公暗中把鲁班的尺子截短了几寸。等工匠们把柱子都锯完了之后，才发现了文公的暗算。这时候，鲁班意识到所有的柱子都太短了，而木料全都用完了。鲁班灵机一动，就把柱子立在了石墩上。这样做不但增加了柱子的美

not only enhanced the aesthetics of the pillars but also made the bases more resilient to rotting. The king was delighted with this innovation. When people asked Lu Ban where he got the brilliant idea, he said, "I have to thank the perfect ruler that Wen Gong gave me!" This slightly shortened ruler was named the Lu Ban ruler, and it remains the gold standard for carpentry today.

In their admiration for Lu Ban, the Chinese people also give credit to the two most important women in his life—his mother and his wife. It is said that the inspiration for the "ink dipper 墨斗," similar to the modern-day "chalk line tool," came from the "powder line bag" used by his mother for sewing. The tool Lu Ban first invented required one person holding each end of the line. At his mother's suggestion, he added a tack to one end of the line, eliminating the need for a second person. To give credit where credit is due, this tack was nicknamed "Ban's mother."

Likewise, Lu Ban's wife inspired the invention of a clamp for holding wood in place on the work bench. This clamp freed her from having to hold the wood herself, so it was nicknamed "Ban's wife." To this day, these two simple tools—"Ban's mother" and "Ban's wife"—are constant reminders to woodworkers of the essential role of mothers and wives in their lives.

In another episode, Lu Ban's wife's love for him led to a gift to the rest of the world. She was just as hardworking as her husband, but she could not bear to see him working under the scorching sun or drenching rain. To enable him to work in comfort under any weather conditions, she invented a "portable pavilion." She later developed this contraption into an essential household item—the umbrella!

In the folklore about Lu Ban, we can see the Chinese people's recognition and appreciation for women's ingenuity and their contribution to men's success.

感，而且可以防止柱脚腐烂。鲁王看了很高兴。人们都问鲁班怎么想出的这个妙招，鲁班说："多亏文公送了我最好的尺子！"后来，人们把截短了的尺子称为鲁班尺，至今仍是木工们的标准尺。

中国人敬仰鲁班，但也把他的部分成就归功于他人生中最重要的两个女人——他的母亲和妻子。据说，鲁班发明"墨斗"（类似于现代的"粉笔线工具"）的灵感来自于母亲缝纫时使用的"粉线袋"。鲁班最初发明的墨斗，两端各需要一个人拿住线头。母亲建议鲁班在一端钉了一颗钉子，这样就不再需要第二个人了。后来，这颗钉子就被昵称为"班母"，以纪念鲁班的母亲。

同样，鲁班发明的一种将木头固定在工作台上的夹子是受到妻子的启发。有了这个夹子，鲁班的妻子就不用自己拿着木头了，所以这种夹子就有了"班妻"的绰号。时至今日，"班母"和"班妻"这两个简单的工具都在时时地提醒着木工们母亲和妻子扮演的重要角色。

还有一个例子，鲁班的妻子对他的爱也惠及了全世界。她和丈夫一样勤劳，但不忍看着丈夫在烈日下、风雨中工作。为了让丈夫在任何天气条件下都能舒适地工作，她发明了一种"活动的亭子"。后来，她把这项发明进化成了每个家庭的必需品——雨伞！

从鲁班的民间传说故事，我们看到中国人非常赞赏女性的聪明才智，以及她们在男性取得的成就中做出的贡献。

Afterword

Unfortunately, new technology is often commandeered by rulers for warfare, sometimes even developed specifically for military use. It is not surprising then that Lu Ban became ensnared in the production of weapons. Fortunately, he was later freed from this entanglement by the great pacifist philosopher Mozi, known for his doctrine of universal love. Lu Ban (507–444 BCE) lived in the early years of the Warring States period, a time of rivalry and conflict among the states. It was also an era of philosophical ferment, when the foundations of China's classical philosophies were laid.

The following event in the life of Lu Ban is documented in the *Book of Mozi*, a philosophical treatise. The king of Chu sought hegemony over all the other states, so he recruited Lu Ban to develop weapons. Soon Lu Ban had invented nine formidable weapons, among them the "cloud ladder" for scaling city walls. The king was now ready to attack the state of Song. When the Song philosopher-cum-official Mozi got wind of this, he rushed to Chu to try and dissuade the king from carrying out this plan. The Chu king would not budge, for he was absolutely certain that Lu Ban's weapons could quickly vanquish the Song state. Finally, Mozi suggested that he and Lu Ban conduct mock battles using models of their respective weapons and a waist belt to represent the city wall. Mozi himself was an expert in military technology, but his focus was on defense. After nine mock battles, Lu Ban's formidable weapons were still unable to break through Mozi's defense. This finally convinced the king of Chu to abandon his war plan.

Another chapter in the *Book of Mozi* tells of a debate between Mozi and Lu Ban about the efficacy of Lu Ban's military devices vs. Mozi's pacifist armament of righteousness. Lu Ban challenged Mozi with these words, "For naval battles, my grappling hook and battering ram can capture and repel the opponent's ships. Does your righteousness have

附 录

令人遗憾的是，统治者常常为了战争而征用新技术，有时甚至为了军事用途专门开发新技术。因此，鲁班身陷兵器制作当中也就不足为奇了。幸亏鲁班后来遇见了主张兼爱与和平的伟大哲学家墨子，将他从制造兵器中解脱了出来。鲁班（公元前507年－公元前444年）生活在战国初期。那是一个诸侯纷争的乱世时代，但也是哲学思想兴起，为中国古典哲学奠基的时代。

哲学著作《墨子》一书中记录了鲁班人生中这样的一个事件。楚王意欲称霸各诸侯国，于是招来鲁班研制兵器。不久，鲁班就发明了九种利器，包括登上城墙的"云梯"。楚王准备好攻打宋国了。宋国哲学家兼士大夫墨子听到这个消息后，急忙赶到了楚国，劝楚王放弃战争。楚王不为所动，因为他确信鲁班的兵器可以助他很快消灭宋国。最后，墨子提议他与鲁班使用各自的兵器，加上一幅腰带作为城墙，进行一场模拟对决。墨子也是一位军事技术专家，但他注重的是防守。鲁班使用自己的兵器发起了九次模拟进攻，还是无法攻破墨子的防守。看到这个结果，楚王终于放弃了发动战争的计划。

《墨子》里另有一篇讲述了墨子与鲁班之间的一场辩论，看看究竟是鲁班的兵器还是墨子主张的正义和平更强大。鲁班先挑战墨子："水上作战，我有钩和拒来对付敌人

something that can do the same?" Mozi replied, "I use love to hook the opponent and respect to repel their attack. If you use the grappling hook and battering ram on your opponent, they can do the same to you. How can the grappling hook and battering ram on your ships be as powerful as the hook and resistance of my righteousness?" With that, Lu Ban was left speechless.

Losing the mock battles and the debate with Mozi led Lu Ban to reconsider his career. In due course, he reoriented his talents back to serving non-military purposes and continued to be as prolific as ever. Among his many inventions, the four below are especially memorable:

- A pedal-powered cycle, a prototype of the modern bicycle
- A kite, called a "wooden bird," that can stay in the air for three days under its own power
- A horse-drawn carriage with a device for the coachman to control the horses
- A lifting device for lowering coffins into their final resting place

Despite the small blemish in Lu Ban's life history recounted above, the dominant image of him in Chinese culture is that of a folk hero. The reverence for Lu Ban's skills is evident in the set phrase "brandishing an ax at Lu Ban's gate," meaning that it is ludicrous to show off one's skill in front of the supreme master Lu Ban. If you hope to truly master Chinese language and culture, this is an excellent set phrase to add to your repertoire. It will come in handy when you wish to gracefully decline a request to perform. You can say "I dare not brandish an ax at Lu Ban's gate," meaning "I dare not show off in front of others who are experts."

的战船，你的正义也有钩和拒吗？"墨子回答说："我用爱来钩，用恭来拒。如果你用钩钩人，别人也可以钩你。你用拒拒人，别人也可以拒你。你船上的钩和拒怎么比得过我的正义呢？"听了这话，鲁班哑口无言了。

模拟战和辩论都输给了墨子以后，鲁班深刻地反省了自己，决定将聪明才智重新投入非军事用途的创造当中，像从前一样创新不止。在鲁班众多的发明当中，以下四项尤其突出：

- 原始的脚踏车
- 一种被称为"木鸟"的风筝，可以靠自身的动力在空中滑翔三天
- 带有马车夫控制马匹装置的马车
- 可以将灵柩放入墓穴的升降装置

尽管鲁班一生中曾有过前面提到的小瑕疵，但他仍然是当之无愧的民族英雄。民间对鲁班的敬仰清楚地体现在"班门弄斧"这个成语中，意思是在鲁班大师面前炫耀自己的能力是个不自量力的举动。如果你希望精通中国语言文化，这个成语很值得学习。当别人请你表现自己而你想婉拒的时候，就可以说"我不敢班门弄斧，"意思是"我不敢在高手面前炫耀自己。"

Vocabulary

1. 负盛名 **fù shèngmíng** prestigious (lit. to carry a great reputation)

2. 冠以···的名字 **guànyǐ...de míngzi** to be named after...; to be crowned with the name of...

3. 工匠 **gōngjiàng** artisan

4. 大师 **dàshī** grandmaster

5. 家喻户晓 **jiāyù hùxiǎo** household name

6. 崇拜 **chóngbài** to worship

7. 祖师爷 **zǔshīyé** patriarch

8. 体现 **tǐxiàn** to reflect, to embody

9. 珍视 **zhēnshì** to value

10. 非凡 **fēifán** extraordinary

11. 特征 **tèzhēng** special characteristic

12. 变害为利 **biànhài wéilì** to turn adversity into advantage

13. 不经意间 **bùjīngyìjiān** inadvertently, unintentionally

14. 开创性 **kāichuàngxìng** pioneering, innovative

15. 证实 **zhèngshí** to confirm

16. 受···之命 **shòu...zhīmìng** to be ordered by..., on the order of...

17. 宫殿 **gōngdiàn** palace

18. 砍伐 **kǎnfá** to cut down (timber)

19. 斧头 **fǔtóu** ax

20. 熟练 **shúliàn** skilled

21. 期限 **qīxiàn** time limit, deadline

22. 抓住 **zhuāzhù** to grab onto

23. 滑倒 **huádǎo** to slip on something slippery

24. 划···口子 **huá...kǒuzi** to cut an opening

25. 锯齿状 **jùchǐzhuàng** serrated, jagged

26. 蝗虫 **huángchóng** locust

27. 坚挺 **jiāntǐng** strong

28. 凑近 **còujìn** get close

29. 下颚 **xià'è** lower jaw

30. 灵感 **línggǎn** inspiration

31. 效率 **xiàolǜ** efficiency

32. 远近闻名 **yuǎnjìn wénmíng** well-known far and near

33. 招来 **zhāolái** to attract, to incur

34. 嫉妒 **jídù** envy

35. 陷害 **xiànhài** to frame, to trump up a charge against

36. 暗中 **ànzhōng** secretly

37. 截短 **jiéduǎn** to truncate

38. 暗算 **ànsuàn** a plot; to plot against

39. 灵机一动 **língjī yídòng** in a flash of inspiration

40. 石墩 **shídūn** stone block

41. 腐烂 **fǔlàn** to rot

42. 妙招 **miàozhāo** brilliant move

43. 多亏 **duōkuī** thanks to

44. 敬仰 **jìngyǎng** to respect

45. 归功于 **guīgōngyú** to be attributed to..., to give credit to...

46. 墨斗 **mòdǒu** ink dipper

47. 缝纫 **féngrèn** sewing

48. 两端 **liǎngduān** both ends

49. 昵称 **nìchēng** nickname

50. 固定 **gùdìng** to stabilize, to affix

51. 夹子 **jiāzi** clip

52. 启发 **qǐfā** inspiration

53. 绰号 **chuòhào** nickname

54. 惠及 **huìjí** to benefit

55. 勤劳 **qínláo** diligent

56. 烈日 **lièrì** scorching sun

57. 舒适 **shūshì** comfortable

58. 亭子 **tíngzi** pavilion

59. 赞赏 **zànshǎng** to appreciate

60. 遗憾 **yíhàn** to regret; something regrettable

61. 征用 **zhēngyòng** to press into service, to deploy

62. 用途 **yòngtú** use, utility

63. 身陷 **shēnxiàn** to fall into a trap

64. 兵器 **bīngqì** weapon

65. 不足为奇 **bùzú wéiqí** not surprising

66. 兼爱 **jiān'ài** universal love

67. 解脱 **jiětuō** to be freed from...

68. 诸侯 **zhūhóu** feudal lords

69. 纷争 **fēnzhēng** dispute, rivalry

70. 兴起 **xīngqǐ** to rise up

71. 奠基 **diànjī** to lay the foundation

72. 意欲 **yìyù** to desire, to be intent on...

73. 称霸 **chēngbà** to dominate

74. 研制 **yánzhì** to develop and make

75. 利器 **lìqì** powerful weapons

76. 登···城墙 **dēng...chéngqiáng** to climb up the city wall

77. 云梯 **yúntī** tall ladder

78. 攻打 **gōngdǎ** to attack

79. 士大夫 **shìdàfū** literati

80. 不为所动 **bù wéi suǒ dòng** unmoved by it

81. 确信 **quèxìn** to firmly believe

82. 消灭 **xiāomiè** to wipe out

83. 腰带 **yāodài** belt

84. 模拟对决 **mónǐ duìjué** mock battle

85. 防守 **fángshǒu** to defend

86. 进攻 **jìngōng** to attack

87. 攻破 **gōngpò** to break through

88. 辩论 **biànlùn** to debate

89. 究竟 **jiūjìng** after all

90. 正义 **zhèngyì** justice, righteousness

91. 钩 **gōu** hook

92. 拒 **jù** ram

93. 恭 **gōng** respect

94. 哑口无言 **yǎkǒu wúyán** speechless

95. 深刻 **shēnkè** deeply; profound

96. 反省 **fǎnxǐng** to reflect

97. 突出 **tūchū** to stand out

98. 滑翔 **huáxiáng** to glide

99. 装置 **zhuāngzhì** device

100. 灵柩 **língjiù** coffin

101. 墓穴 **mùxué** coffin pit, grave

102. 升降 **shēngjiàng** to lift and to lower (like an elevator)

103. 瑕疵 **xiácī** flaw

104. 当之无愧 **dāngzhī wúkuì** to fully deserve, to be worthy of

105. 班门弄斧 **Bān mén nòngfǔ** a set phrase meaning "to brandish an ax at the gate of Master Ban"

106. 炫耀 **xuànyào** to show off

107. 不自量力 **búzì liànglì** to be unaware of one's own limitations

108. 举动 **jǔdòng** action, a move

109. 精通 **jīngtōng** to master something; highly proficient

110. 婉拒 **wǎnjù** to decline politely

Questions for contemplation and discussion

1. From the two very different portrayals of Lu Ban in folklore and in the *Book of Mozi*, what is your image of the historical Lu Ban?

2. Lu Ban has been called China's Leonardo DaVinci. Do you agree with that assessment? Are there other inventors in the Western world who are comparable to Lu Ban?

3. Can you think of other examples of unintended consequences of cutting-edge technology being deployed for military purposes?

4. As a modern, culturally sophisticated person, what do you think of Lu Ban's mother and wife?

5. To enhance your learning of Chinese, think of a scenario in which the set phrase "brandishing an ax at Lu Ban's gate" can be used as a clincher.

Two Virtuous Mothers
of Ancient China

A vexing question for parents in every culture is how to raise their children to become good and successful citizens. Some Westerners assume that there is a traditional Chinese way of raising children, but in fact there has always been much debate and no consensus on this, as demonstrated by aphorisms representing different points of view. Two such aphorisms are "fathers should be stern, and mothers should be benevolent" and "benevolent mothers beget prodigal sons." In this story we will see how these different points of view play out in practice.

慈母与虎妈

古今中外，如何把孩子<u>培养成优秀</u>的公民是所有父母都<u>为之</u><u>烦恼</u>的问题。可能有些西方人以为中国人有一种<u>养育</u>孩子的传统方式，其实在这个问题上，中国人也一直<u>争论不休</u>，并没有<u>共识</u>。人们不同的观点也有不同的<u>格言来表述</u>，如"<u>严父慈母</u>"和"<u>慈母多败儿</u>"。在下面的两个故事里，我们将看到这些格言是怎样<u>呈现</u>在现实生活中的。

The great humanist philosopher Mencius lost his father when he was just three years old, and he was raised solely by his widowed mother. Despite being poor, she was determined to provide Mencius with a secure happy home and a good education. She managed to eke out a bare-bones living by weaving cloth, but she could only afford to live in a humble home in a very undesirable location—right next to a graveyard. Mencius was a very smart boy, and his play was preparation for adult life. Even at the age of three, he quickly learned to do the things he saw adults doing. Soon his favorite play became burial rituals. He would happily build grave mounds and chant mourning songs. His mother quickly decided that this was no place to raise her son, so she moved to an area next to the marketplace. Soon Mencius started talking like glib businessmen, boasting about their goods and haggling with customers. His mother was again disenchanted, but this time she took her time investigating other options. She finally chose a small old hut next to a school and turned it into a simple cozy home for Mencius. Soon Mencius started behaving like a cultivated scholar. His mother finally relaxed and thought, "This is where I can raise my son."

Although Mencius's mother had to be extremely frugal, she would spare no cost in teaching Mencius a lesson. One day when they were still living near the marketplace, Mencius was upset at hearing their neighbor slaughter a pig he had raised, so he asked his mother why. She was preoccupied at the loom, so she said offhandedly, "So you'd have some meat to eat." But as soon as she said it, she realized that she could never afford to buy meat, and what she had said was simply good-humored wishful thinking. But to a five-year-old it would probably sound like a promise, and if she did not fulfill that promise Mencius would feel she had deceived him. Not having meat to eat is no big deal, but having Mencius learn dishonest behavior would be a tragedy. In the end, she bought a small piece of meat and cooked it for Mencius.

孟子是中国伟大的人文主义哲学家。他刚满三岁的时候，父亲就去世了，因此他是由母亲一个人抚养长大的。虽然家里很穷，但母亲决心给孟子创造一个安全幸福的家庭环境，并让他受到良好的教育。孟母靠织布勉强维持生活。因为比较理想地段的房子都太贵了，他们只好在墓地的旁边找了个住处。孟子是个非常聪明的孩子，他玩的游戏都是为将来成人的生活做准备的。才三岁的孟子看到大人们做的事情，很快就学会了。不久，他最喜欢的游戏就是葬礼。他常堆一个坟冢，唱着哀歌，自己玩得不亦乐乎。孟子的母亲很快就发现这里不是养育孩子的地方，所以就搬到了一个集市的附近。没过多久，孟子就开始像那些油嘴滑舌的商人一样，吹嘘他们的商品，跟顾客们讨价还价。孟子的母亲又感到很失望，但这次她多花了一些时间看了看周边的住房，最终选择了学校附近的一个破旧小屋，并将它变成了一个简朴温馨的家。很快，孟子的言行就变得像一个有修养的学者了。母亲终于放心地说："这才是我可以抚养儿子长大的地方。"

　　孟子的母亲非常节俭，但在教育孟子的时候从不吝惜。他们还住在集市附近的时候，有一天，孟子听见邻居屠宰了一头自己养大的猪就很难过，问母亲邻居为什么要这样做。母亲正忙着织布，就随口答道："这样你就可以有一点肉吃了。"话一出口，母亲就意识到自己刚说的那句话只是一个愿望而已，实际上他们一向是吃不起肉的。不过，那句话对一个五岁的孩子来说就是一个承诺。要是母亲食言了，孟子就会觉得被妈妈骗了。没有肉吃不要紧，但让孟子学会不诚实的行为就是一个悲剧了。最后，母亲还是买了一小块肉煮给孟子吃了。

One day, on his way to school, Mencius decided to play hooky and go play with other kids outside. When he got home, his mother was working at her loom as usual. Seeing the dirt on his clothes, she knew what had happened, but she asked him, "Did you just get out of school?" Mencius replied, "No, I would never tell a lie. I went to play with other kids today." She said, "Come closer, I want to show you something." She picked up a pair of scissors and cut across the cloth on the loom. Then she said, "You see what just happened to this piece of cloth? It took me a long time to get this far, but now it is totally useless. This is not something we can afford to do! Your skipping school is like what I just did." From this example, Mencius learned the lesson of "quitting halfway" in the most powerful but gentle way possible.[1]

Mencius eventually became one of the greatest scholars of his time. With his mother's parenting style, he grew to view mankind as innately good and the world as naturally benign. However, the realities of his time—the Warring States period—flew in the face of this worldview. He aspired to find a ruler who would listen to his humanistic teachings and put them into practice, perhaps even usher in a new, peaceful dynasty. After traveling for many years and having many audiences with various rulers, Mencius was finally retained by the king of Qi. For a while it seemed that his long-cherished dream might come true. But soon the king of Qi waged war against a neighboring state, and it became clear to Mencius that the king had used him to mask his own aggression. In despair, Mencius realized that he could never be the philosopher standing behind a good ruler, so he gave up his career as a political adviser. He was not particularly successful in his own eyes, but posthumously he came to be regarded as a Confucian sage, second only to Confucius himself.

---

[1] "Quitting halfway" is a favorite aphorism in China. The episode of cutting a piece of half-finished cloth on the loom appears in other folktales as well, as can be seen in the next story in this book.

有一天，孟子在上学的路上看见其他的小朋友在外面玩，就决定逃学，跟他们一起去玩了。他回家的时候，妈妈像平常一样在忙着织布。看到孟子衣服上都是土，妈妈心里什么都明白了，不过她还是问孟子："你刚放学吗？"孟子回答说："我从来不撒谎，今天没上学，跟小朋友们出去玩了。"妈妈又说："儿啊，你过来，我给你看样东西。"妈妈拿起一把剪刀，一下子把织布机上的布料剪开了，然后说："你看这块布，我花了很长时间才织成这样，现在完全废了吧？我们可不能这样啊！你逃学就像我刚才把织好的布剪了一样。"妈妈现身说法，以最有力又最温柔的方式让孟子明白了不能半途而废的道理[1]。

孟子最终成为了古代最伟大的学者之一。在母亲的养育下，孟子从小就相信人性本善，世界是美好的。然而，他生活在战国时期，社会现实与他本人的世界观是背道而驰的。孟子渴望找到一位君王，接受自己的仁政主张，甚至于开创一个太平盛世的王朝。孟子周游列国多年，游说过多位君王以后，终于为齐王所留用。当时孟子感觉自己长久以来的梦想似乎就要实现了。但没过多久，齐王就对邻国发动了战争，这样一来，孟子看清了齐王原来只是利用他的主张来伪装自己的野心，随即就意识到自己这一生不可能实现辅佐一位明君的梦想了。失望之余，他主动结束了自己的从政生涯。孟子在有生之年没有实现自己的抱负，但去世之后被尊为儒家圣人，地位仅次于孔子。

---

[1] "半途而废"是一个很常用的成语。将织布机上的半成品剪开的那一幕也出现在其他的民间传说中，在本书的下一章中也可以看到。

Afterword

During the Han Dynasty there was another widowed mother who took the opposite approach to child-rearing to that of Mencius's mother. Her claim to fame is raising her son Han Boyu to become a paragon of filial piety. Han Boyu lost his father at a young age, so his mother felt it was up to her to fill the role of the disciplinarian father. She had a strong will of her own and had high expectations for her son. Being a spirited boy, Boyu naturally had his mischievous moments. If he slacked off in his studies, or misbehaved in any way, his mother would beat him with a cane. Boyu knew that his mother punished him for his own good, so he never protested or even cried. Instead, he would kneel to receive his punishment and apologize to his mother for his misdeed. As he grew up, he became very self-disciplined and always held his mother close to his heart. Every time he came home, he would bring her something good to eat to show his love.

When Boyu was in his fifties, he made a mistake that made his mother angry. For the first time in many years, she picked up the cane to beat Boyu. As before, Boyu knelt to take his punishment but within seconds he put both hands to his face and started crying. Perplexed by her son's unusual reaction, she said, "My son, I have never seen you cry before. Did I hit you too hard this time?" Boyu raised his head and replied, "Ma, it's not that you hit me too hard. In the past whenever you beat me, I could feel your strength and knew you were strong and healthy. This time I didn't feel any pain, so I realized that you are now old and frail. I feel so sad that we won't be together much longer." At those words, mother and son wept in each other's arms.

The influence Boyu's mother had on him lasted well after her death. The story goes that he went through a period of depression after his mother died, during which he began spending a lot of time with idle, worthless people drinking and gambling with them. In desperation, his wife thought of a way to turn him around. She went looking for him

附 录

汉朝时期，另一位守寡母亲的育儿方法与孟母的截然相反。这位母亲之所以出名，是因为她把儿子韩伯俞抚养成了遵守孝道的典范。韩伯俞幼年丧父，母亲觉得自己应该承担起严父的责任。她意志坚强，对儿子也有很高的期望。伯俞是个活泼好动的孩子，自然有调皮捣蛋的时候。只要伯俞不好好学习，或是行为不端，母亲就会用手杖打他一顿。伯俞知道母亲惩罚他是为了他好，所以从来不反抗，甚至不曾哭过。相反，他会跪在地上，接受母亲的惩罚，并为他的错误行为向母亲道歉。长大以后，伯俞非常自律，总是惦念着母亲。每次回家，伯俞都给母亲带些好吃的东西，以表达对母亲的爱。

伯俞50多岁的时候，有一次做错了事情，母亲很生气。她很多年没打过伯俞了，这一次又操起手杖打了儿子。伯俞像以前一样跪在地上，接受母亲的惩罚。只过了几秒钟，他就双手捂脸哭了起来。母亲很诧异，就问道："儿啊，你以前挨打从来没哭过，这次是不是我打得太重了？"伯俞抬起头来说："娘，不是您打得太重了。以前您打我的时候，我能感觉到您的力量，就知道您强壮健康。这次，我一点儿都没感觉到痛，才知道您老了，身体虚弱无力了。想到咱们在一起的日子不多了，就很难过。"说完，母子俩相拥而泣。

伯俞母亲去世后，对他依然有威慑力。据说，伯俞在母亲去世后消沉了一段时间，开始跟一些不三不四的人混在一起，喝酒赌博。伯俞的妻子实在受不了了，就想出了一个办

dressed in her deceased mother-in-law's outfit and carrying her cane. As she approached Boyu, he thought he saw the ghost of his mother and was jolted back to the right path.

You may be surprised to learn that these two very different stories of widowed mothers came from the same author, the Han Dynasty scholar official Liu Xiang (77–6 BCE). The story of Mencius's mother is one of 110 biographies in the anthology *Biographies of Exemplary Women*. The story of Han Boyu and his mother is from the *Garden of Talks*. In both stories, the author adopts a non-judgmental tone, thus leaving the moral of the stories to the reader's imagination.

Vocabulary

1. 培养 **péiyǎng** to nurture

2. 优秀 **yōuxiù** excellent

3. 为之烦恼 **wèi zhī fánnǎo** to worry about

4. 养育 **yǎngyù** to bring up (a child)

5. 争论不休 **zhēnglùn bùxiū** to debate endlessly

6. 共识 **gòngshí** consensus

7. 格言 **géyán** motto

8. 表述 **biǎoshù** to express

9. 严父慈母 **yánfù címǔ** strict father and kindly mother

10. 慈母多败儿 **címǔ duō bài'ér** many kindly mothers beget wastrel sons

11. 呈现 **chéngxiàn** to manifest

12. 人文主义 **rénwén zhǔyì** humanism

13. 哲学家 **zhéxuéjiā** philosopher

14. 抚养 **fǔyǎng** to bring up

15. 织布 **zhībù** to weave cloth

16. 勉强 **miǎnqiǎng** barely, reluctantly

17. 墓地 **mùdì** cemetery

18. 葬礼 **zànglǐ** funeral

19. 坟冢 **fénzhǒng** tomb

20. 哀歌 **āigē** dirge

21. 不亦乐乎 **bú yì lè hū** really happy (lit. isn't that a happy thing?)

22. 集市 **jíshì** market

23. 油嘴滑舌 **yóuzuǐ huáshé** glib (lit. oily mouth and slick tongue)

法来让丈夫振作起来。她穿上婆婆生前的衣服，拿着她的手杖。当她走近伯俞时，他以为看见了母亲的鬼魂，一下子就把他拉回到正道上了。

这两篇守寡母亲的故事尽管截然不同，但却出自同一位作者，汉代文官刘向（公元前77年－公元前6年）。孟母的故事是《列女传》110篇传记中的一篇，而韩伯俞和母亲的故事来自《说苑》。在这两篇故事中，作者都采取了非评判的语气，从而将故事的寓意留给读者去想象了。

24. 吹嘘 chuīxū to brag

25. 讨价还价 tǎojià huánjià to bargain

26. 失望 shīwàng to be disappointed

27. 温馨 wēnxīn warm and cozy

28. 言行 yánxíng words and deeds

29. 修养 xiūyǎng (personal) cultivation

30. 节俭 jiéjiǎn frugal

31. 吝惜 lìnxī stingy

32. 屠宰 túzǎi to slaughter

33. 意识到 yìshi dào to realize

34. 承诺 chéngnuò promise

35. 食言 shíyán to renege on a promise (lit. to eat words)

36. 骗 piàn to deceive

37. 行为 xíngwéi behavior

38. 悲剧 bēijù tragedy

39. 逃学 táoxué to play truant from school

40. 撒谎 sāhuǎng to lie

41. 布料 bùliào fabric

42. 废 fèi to waste

43. 现身说法 xiànshēn shuōfǎ to explain a truth by one's own action

44. 温柔 wēnróu gentle

45. 半途而废 bàntú ér fèi to quit halfway

46. 人性本善 rénxìng běnshàn human nature is good

47. 世界观 shìjièguān worldview

48. 背道而驰 **bèidào ér chí** to run in opposite directions

49. 仁政主张 **rénzhèng zhǔzhāng** proposition of benevolent governance

50. 开创 **kāichuàng** to create, to open up

51. 太平盛世 **tàipíng shèngshì** peaceful and prosperous era

52. 周游列国 **zhōuyóu lièguó** travel around the world

53. 游说 **yóushuì** to lobby, to persuade (rulers)

54. 伪装 **wěizhuāng** to camouflage

55. 野心 **yěxīn** ambition (perjorative)

56. 随即 **suíjí** thereupon

57. 辅佐 **fǔzuǒ** to assist

58. 明君 **míngjūn** enlightened ruler

59. 从政 **cóngzhèng** to engage in politics

60. 生涯 **shēngyá** career

61. 有生之年 **yǒushēng zhī nián** lifetime

62. 抱负 **bàofù** aspiration

63. 尊为 **zūnwéi** to revered (someone) as...

64. 儒家圣人 **rújiā shèngrén** Confucian sage

65. 仅次于 **jǐn cìyú** second only to

66. 守寡 **shǒuguǎ** to be a widow (i.e. not remarry)

67. 截然 **jiérán** sharply

68. 之所以···是因为 **zhī suǒyǐ... shì yīnwèi** the reason why...is because...

69. 遵守 **zūnshǒu** to follow, to obey

70. 孝道 **xiàodào** filial piety

71. 典范 **diǎnfàn** model

72. 幼年丧父 **yòunián sàngfù** to lose one's father at a young age

73. 承担 **chéngdān** to bear (responsibility)

74. 意志坚强 **yìzhì jiānqiáng** to have a strong will

75. 活泼好动 **huópō hàodòng** lively and active

76. 调皮捣蛋 **tiáopí dǎodàn** mischievous, rambunctious

77. 行为不端 **xíngwéi bùduān** to misbehave

78. 手杖 **shǒuzhàng** cane

79. 惩罚 **chéngfá** to punish

80. 跪 **guì** to kneel

81. 道歉 **dàoqiàn** to apologize

82. 自律 **zìlǜ** self-discipline

83. 惦念 **diànniàn** to remember (someone) with concern

84. 操起 **cāoqǐ** to pick up, to grab

85. 捂脸 **wǔliǎn** to cover one's face

86. 诧异 **chàyì** to be surprised

87. 挨打 **áidǎ** to be beaten

88. 虚弱无力 **xūruò wúlì** weak and have no strength

89. 相拥而泣 **xiāngyōng ér qì** to embrace and cry

90. 威慑力 **wēishèlì** power to intimidate

91. 消沉 **xiāochén** depressed

92. 不三不四 **bùsān búsì** ne'er-do-well, dubious

93. 混 **hùn** to mix with, to hang out with

94. 赌博 **dǔbó** to gamble

95. 振作 **zhènzuò** to boost up

96. 鬼魂 **guǐhún** ghost

97. 正道 **zhèngdào** righteous path

98. 列女传 **Liènǚ Zhuàn** Biography of Women

99. 传记 **zhuànjì** biography

100. 说苑 **Shuōyuàn** Garden of Talks

101. 非评判 **fēi píngpàn** non-judgmental

102. 寓意 **yùyì** implication, moral message

Questions for contemplation and discussion

1. Have you heard of the book *Battle Hymn of the Tiger Mother* by the law professor Amy Chua? If so, what do you think of it? If you have not read it, what can you infer from the title of the book?

2. Can you describe the environment in which you grew up? How big a factor do you think it was in shaping the person you have become?

3. What is your impression of Chinese parents' way of raising their children?

4. Do you agree with the contemporary view that corporal punishment under any circumstances is harmful? If so, why has it persisted in so many cultures in the past and present?

5. What is your honest opinion of the Chinese concept of filial piety?

The Virtuous Wife

The aphorism "behind every great man is a great woman" is not just a modern Western notion. It is also a belief cherished by the Chinese since ancient times, and we have the following story to illustrate it.

During the Han Dynasty there was a happy-go-lucky fellow by the name of Yue Yangzi. What we know about him is mostly through the heroic deeds of his wife. Yangzi was very fortunate to have a loving mother and wife, even more so that the three of them lived in harmony.

乐羊子妻

"每个成功的男人背后都有一位伟大的女性"这句格言不只是西方人的观念，也是中国人自古以来就珍视的信念。下面这篇故事可以证实这个说法。

汉朝时期，有个名叫乐羊子的人，整天逍遥自在，无忧无虑。我们对他的了解，主要是通过他贤惠又勇敢的妻子。羊子很幸运，因为他家有慈母爱妻，况且他们三人相处得非常和睦。

One day Yangzi found a gold ingot on the street. He took it to his wife thinking that she would be delighted. But what he got from his wife was a gentle scolding: "Yangzi, I know you would like be a better provider for your family, but think about the person who lost that ingot." That was enough to make Yangzi return to the spot where he found the ingot and wait for its owner to come retrieve it.

Soon after this incident, Yangzi realized that he needed to make something of himself, so he left home to pursue an education. Although he soon began missing all the comforts of home, he persevered for a while. A year later, he could not bear his homesickness anymore and returned home. His wife and mother could not believe their eyes when they saw him coming back so soon. At first, they were ecstatic, and his wife prepared a sumptuous dinner with all his favorite comfort foods. Over dinner, as they chatted about Yangzi's recent life and his future plans, it dawned on his wife that he had abandoned his studies! Without a word his wife walked over to her loom with a pair of scissors and cut the half-completed silk cloth straight across. Yangzi was alarmed by this reckless act, so he asked her why she had done it. She remained calm as she explained: "I've been weaving this piece of cloth day and night for almost a year. It took several months to raise the silkworms and extract the silk, another month to reel the raw silk into threads, then every day, from morning till night, I've sat at the loom weaving this silk cloth inch by inch. Now it has become totally useless. An education is even more precious than a piece of silk, and it can only be achieved through perseverance. Think about it, isn't abandoning your education just like what I did with this cloth? But we are happy to see you, so let's just enjoy our little reunion tonight." The next morning Yangzi again embarked on his journey to seek an education, and this time he did not return home for seven years.

有一天，羊子在街上捡到一块金元宝。他把金元宝带回家交给了妻子，以为她会很高兴。没想到妻子略带责备地说："羊子，我知道你想让咱们过得更好，但你应该设身处地，替丢失这块金元宝的人想一想。"听了妻子的话，羊子回到捡金元宝的地方，等着失主回来。

这件事发生后不久，羊子意识到他应该有所作为，于是就离家求学去了。没过多久，他开始想念家里舒适的生活，但还是坚持了一段时间。一年后，他实在受不了就回家了。他的妻子和母亲看到他这么快就回家来了，真不敢相信。一开始，她们欢天喜地，他的妻子还准备了一顿丰盛的晚餐，做了他爱吃的所有家乡菜给他接风。吃晚饭的时候，他们聊到羊子最近的生活和未来的打算，妻子才明白原来丈夫竟然放弃了学业！妻子一言不发，拿起一把剪刀走到织布机旁边，把织了一半的布料剪开了。羊子见了大吃一惊，就问她这是干什么。妻子平静地说："这块布料我日以继夜地织了快一年了。养蚕抽丝要几个月，缫丝又要一个月，然后，每天从早到晚我都坐在织布机前一寸一寸地织这块布料，现在完全废了。受教育比这块丝绸还要珍贵，只有持之以恒才能达成目标。你想，放弃学业不就像我刚才把布料剪了一样吗？不过，见到你还是很开心，今晚咱们就好好吃个团圆饭吧！"第二天，羊子又踏上了求学的征程，这次，他一去就七年都没回家。

Once during those seven years a neighbor's hen wandered into their yard. Yangzi's mother caught it and made it into a special treat for dinner. At the dinner table, Yangzi's wife couldn't pick up her chopsticks. Instead, tears started falling into her bowl. When her mother-in-law asked what was troubling her, she replied, "We've come through many hard times since Yangzi left home, but I'm grateful that we've never had to go hungry. What I see on the table tonight is only our neighbor's misfortune. How can I possibly enjoy it?" Even before she had finished speaking, her mother-in-law started tearing up too. There was no way for this episode to end well. The best the mother-in-law could do was to offer the stewed hen to beggars on the street.

As you can imagine, two women in such a precarious situation could easily fall prey to criminals. Sure enough, one day a thug broke into their home intending to rape the young wife, but he ran into the mother-in-law first, so he grabbed both her hands behind her back. Hearing the screams of her mother-in-law, the wife ran out with her kitchen knife. The thug scoffed at her, "If you want to save your mother-in-law's life, put down your knife and come with me. I'll spare both your lives. Otherwise, your husband will never see his mother again!" At that the wife looked up to heaven and let out a deep sigh, then without any warning drew the knife across her throat and collapsed to the ground. Not to be caught with blood on his hands, the thug vanished in a flash. Shocked by this heinous crime, the entire town rallied to hunt down the thug. In no time he was caught and beheaded in the public square. To honor the martyred wife, the magistrate ordered the finest silk burial regalia for her, held the most majestic funeral, and bestowed upon her the posthumous title of "Chaste Righteousness."

在那七年里，有一次邻居家的母鸡溜进了他们家的院子里。羊子的母亲抓住了母鸡，做了一道美味的晚餐。吃饭的时候，羊子的妻子拿不起筷子，眼泪不由自主地掉进了她的碗里。婆婆问她怎么了，羊子妻子回答道："羊子走了以后，我们吃了很多苦，但我很感恩我们从没挨过饿。在今晚的餐桌上，我看到的只是邻居的不幸。我怎么可能享受这顿晚餐呢？"话还没说完，婆婆也哭了起来。现在也没什么补救的好办法了，婆婆只能把炖好的母鸡端给街上的乞丐们享用了。

可想而知，相依为命的婆媳二人很容易成为坏人的目标。果然，有一天，一个恶棍闯进了他们家，想要奸污年轻的媳妇，不过，他先撞见了婆婆，就将她的双手扭到了背后。听见婆婆的尖叫声，媳妇从厨房抓起一把菜刀冲了出来。恶棍冷笑道："想救你婆婆的命，就放下菜刀跟我走，我就饶了你们俩的性命。不然，你先生就再也见不到他母亲了。"听了这话，媳妇抬起头，仰天长叹了一声，不露声色地举起菜刀划过自己的脖颈，猝然倒地了。恶棍见状，因为害怕自己手上沾满鲜血被逮住，赶紧逃之夭夭了。镇上的人听到这起惨案都很震惊，大家齐心协力追捕恶棍。不一会儿，恶棍就被逮住并带到广场上砍了头。为了纪念英勇献身的妻子，太守为她订制了最精美的丝绸寿衣，举办了最隆重的葬礼，并追授她"贞义"的谥号。

Commentary

This story first appeared in the "Biographies of Exemplary Women" section of *History of the Later Han Dynasty* (25–220 CE) by the historian Fan Ye (398–445 CE). Presumably, the story has some historical basis. However, the hero of the story is known only as Yue Yangzi's wife, for even the author-historian did not know her name. But by including this nameless woman of humble origins in the official history, he has memorialized her in the Chinese popular consciousness.

Modern readers may find the martyrdom of the virtuous wife in this story hard to believe, perhaps even absurd. They may wish to change the ending of the story to one in which she emerges from the dilemma more like our version of a hero rather than a victim. But let us consider the case in its historical context.

Historically, in many Asian cultures, suicide under certain circumstances is considered an honorable act, one that brings dignity to the person and even revenge to the offender. In China the concept of "sacrificing life for righteousness" was given a philosophical foundation by the humanist philosopher Mencius (372–289 BCE). Below is a famous passage from the *Book of Mencius*:

> I like fish, and I also like bear paws. If I cannot have both, then I'll take the bear paws and forego the fish. Life is also something that I crave, and righteousness too. But if I cannot have both, then I will choose righteousness over life. While I crave life, there is something I crave even more than life, therefore I would not sacrifice that something of greater value in order to hold on to life. Death is something that I abhor, but there is something I abhor even more than death. Therefore, there are certain perils that I would not evade in order to avoid death.... It's not only the virtuous among us who have this mentality; we all have it. The only

评论

上面的这篇故事最早出现在史学家范晔（398年–445年）的《后汉书·列女传》中。想必这个故事是有一些历史依据的。然而，故事主人公的真实姓名连史学家也不知道，只称她为乐羊子妻。不过，将这位出生贫寒的女性无名氏载入正史，中国百姓就都熟知乐羊子妻的故事了。

对于现代读者来说，贤良的妻子自我献身的故事也许看起来不可思议，甚至有些荒唐。也许有人希望重写故事的结尾，比如，把她从一个受害者变成一个超能的自卫英雄。然而，让我们在历史的背景下来评议这个故事吧。

在许多亚洲国家的传统文化中，个人在某种困境下自杀被视为一种高尚的行为，可以为个人带来尊严，甚至可以报复对手。在中国，"舍生取义"这个观念最早是由人文主义哲学家孟子（公元前372年 – 公元前289年）阐释的。《孟子》中有以下这段名言：

> 我喜欢吃鱼，也喜欢吃熊掌。如果我不能两者兼得，那我就会放弃鱼而选择吃熊掌。生是我渴求的，义也是我渴求的。假如只能选择一个，那我会舍生而取义。虽然我渴求生，但还有比生更重要的事情，因此我不会选择苟且偷生。我厌恶死，但还有比死更让我厌恶的事情。因此，有些险恶我不会为了保全性命而逃避。…这种理念不只是圣贤才

difference is, the virtuous among us can prevent the loss of this mentality.

An important aspect of Mencius's philosophy, expressed in the final two sentences, is that "sacrificing life for righteousness" is not only the virtuous thing to do but it also accords with human nature. This optimistic view of human nature had plenty of detractors in Mencius's time and throughout history.[1] Mencius did recognize the existence of evil, but believed that it arises from the loss of innate goodness.

Returning to Yue Yangzi's wife, at the moment when she was threatened by the thug, she had four options: stand by while the thug kidnaps her mother-in-law, cooperate with the thug and be raped, try to kill the thug with the knife—with a likely disastrous outcome—or commit honor suicide. With little time to weigh these options, she followed her gut instinct. If she had embraced Mencius's philosophy, she would have felt immeasurable comfort in her final moments.

---

[1] According to Xunzi (300–230 BCE), another well-respected philosopher of the Confucian school, mankind is inherently evil, and it is only through moral cultivation that one overcomes this evil.

有，我们每个人都有，而唯一不同的是圣贤不会丢弃这种理念。

这段话的最后两句表述了孟子哲学一个很重要的方面，即"舍生取义"不仅是仁义之事，而且符合人性。这种对人性的乐观看法自从孟子时代以来一直都存在争议[1]。虽然孟子承认恶是存在的，但相信只有丧失了天生的善，恶才会出现。

回到乐羊子妻子的情况，在被恶棍威胁的那一刻，她有四个选择：旁观恶棍绑架婆婆；顺从恶棍而被强奸；拿着刀试图杀死恶棍呢，那后果势必不堪设想；或者为了贞义而自杀。那一刻，她没有时间考虑，凭着直觉做了选择。如果她是遵从孟子的哲学，也许会在结束自己生命的那一刻感到莫大的安慰。

---

[1] 另一位备受尊敬的儒家哲学家荀子(公元前300年 – 公元前230年)认为，人性本恶，只有通过道德修养才能克服这种恶。

Vocabulary

1. 珍视 **zhēnshì** to cherish, to value
2. 信念 **xìnniàn** belief
3. 证实 **zhèngshí** to confirm
4. 逍遥自在 **xiāoyáo zìzài** carefree
5. 无忧无虑 **wúyōu wúlǜ** without a care in the world
6. 贤惠 **xiánhuì** (re women) virtuous
7. 慈母爱妻 **címǔ àiqī** loving mother and loving wife
8. 况且 **kuàngqiě** moreover
9. 和睦 **hémù** harmonious
10. 金元宝 **jīnyuánbǎo** gold ingot
11. 略 **lüè** slightly
12. 责备 **zébèi** to reprove
13. 设身处地 **shèshēn chǔdì** to put yourself in the situation
14. 失主 **shīzhǔ** owner who lost something
15. 有所作为 **yǒusuǒ zuòwéi** to make something of oneself
16. 坚持 **jiānchí** to persevere
17. 欢天喜地 **huāntiān xǐdì** overjoyed
18. 丰盛 **fēngshèng** sumptuous
19. 接风 **jiēfēng** to give a welcoming reception
20. 竟然 **jìngrán** as it turns out, unexpectedly
21. 放弃 **fàngqì** to give up
22. 织布机 **zhībùjī** loom (cloth-weaving machine)
23. 日以继夜 **rì yǐ jì yè** day and night
24. 抽丝 **chōusī** to reel silk floss from silkworm cocoons
25. 缫丝 **sāosī** to reel silk floss into thread
26. 持之以恒 **chízhī yǐhéng** to persevere over a long period of time
27. 团圆饭 **tuányuánfàn** reunion dinner
28. 踏上···征程 **tàshàng…zhēngchéng** to embark on a journey of...
29. 不由自主 **bùyóu zìzhǔ** involuntarily, cannot help but...
30. 感恩 **gǎn'ēn** grateful
31. 挨···饿 **ái…è** to suffer hunger
32. 补救 **bǔjiù** to remedy
33. 端 **duān** to carry in both hands

34. 乞丐 **qǐgài** beggar

35. 可想而知 **kě xiǎng ér zhī** as can be imagined

36. 相依为命 **xiāngyī wéimìng** to lean on each other for survival

37. 婆媳 **póxí** mother-in-law and daughter-in-law

38. 恶棍 **ègùn** scoundrel

39. 奸污 **jiānwū** to rape

40. 撞见 **zhuàngjiàn** to bump into

41. 扭 **niǔ** to twist

42. 尖叫 **jiānjiào** to scream

43. 冷笑 **lěngxiào** to sneer

44. 救…命 **jiù…mìng** to save a life

45. 饶…性命 **ráo…xìngmìng** to spare…life (also 饶命 to spare a life)

46. 仰天长叹 **yǎngtiān chángtàn** to sigh toward heaven

47. 不露声色 **búlù shēngsè** unobtrusively, in a low-key way

48. 划 **huá** to draw across, to slice

49. 脖颈 **bójǐng** neck

50. 猝然 **cùrán** suddenly

51. 见状 **jiànzhuàng** to see the situation

52. 沾满 **zhānmǎn** dripping in, stained with

53. 逮住 **dǎizhù** to catch (a fleeing person or animal)

54. 逃之夭夭 **táozhī yāoyāo** to have escaped, nowhere to be found

55. 惨案 **cǎn'àn** murder, slaying

56. 震惊 **zhènjīng** shocked

57. 齐心协力 **qíxīn xiélì** to work unitedly

58. 追捕 **zhuībǔ** to hunt down

59. 砍…头 **kǎn…tóu** to chop off the head, to behead

60. 献身 **xiànshēn** to sacrifice oneself

61. 太守 **tàishǒu** prefect, magistrate

62. 寿衣 **shòuyī** shroud

63. 隆重 **lóngzhòng** grandiose

64. 葬礼 **zànglǐ** funeral

65. 追授 **zhuīshòu** to award posthumously

66. 贞义 **zhēnyì** chastity

67. 谥号 **shìhào** posthumous title

68. 想必 **xiǎngbì** presumably

69. 依据 **yījù** basis, documentation

70. 主人公 **zhǔréngōng** protagonist, hero

71. 贫寒 **pínhán** poor

72. 无名氏 **wúmíngshì** anonymous

73. 载入正史 **zǎirù zhèngshǐ** to be recorded in official history

74. 熟知 **shúzhī** to be familiar with

75. 自我献身 **zìwǒ xiànshēn** to sacrifice oneself

76. 不可思议 **bùkě sīyì** unthinkable, unbelievable

77. 荒唐 **huāngtáng** absurd

78. 结尾 **jiéwěi** conclusion, end

79. 超能 **chāonéng** supremely capable

80. 自卫英雄 **zìwèi yīngxióng** self-defense hero

81. 评议 **píngyì** to critique

82. 困境 **kùnjìng** predicament

83. 高尚 **gāoshàng** noble, lofty

84. 尊严 **zūnyán** dignity

85. 报复 **bàofù** to revenge

86. 舍生取义 **shěshēng qǔyì** to sacrifice life for righteousness

87. 阐释 **chǎnshì** to explain

88. 熊掌 **xióngzhǎng** bear paw

89. 两者兼得 **liǎngzhě jiāndé** to have both

90. 放弃 **fàngqì** to abandon, to give up

91. 渴求 **kěqiú** to yearn for

92. 苟且偷生 **gǒuqiě tōushēng** to drag out a shameful life

93. 厌恶 **yànwù** to hate

94. 险恶 **xiǎn'è** danger

95. 保全 **bǎoquán** to preserve

96. 圣贤 **shèngxián** sage

97. 丢弃 **diūqì** to throw away, to lose

98. 表述 **biǎoshù** to express

99. 仁义 **rényì** benevolence and righteousness

100. 争议 **zhēngyì** to dispute; controversy

101. 承认 **chéngrèn** to admit

102. 丧失 **sàngshī** to lose

103. 威胁 **wēixié** to threaten; a threat

104. 旁观 **pángguān** to be a bystander

105. 绑架 **bǎngjià** to kidnap

106. 顺从 **shùncóng** to obey, to comply with

107. 强奸 **qiángjiān** to rape

108. 势必 **shìbì** bound to

109. 不堪设想 **bùkān shèxiǎng** too dreadful to contemplate

110. 凭着直觉 **píngzhe zhíjué** instinctively

111. 遵从 **zūncóng** to follow

112. 莫大 **mòdà** greatest (none greater)

113. 安慰 **ānwèi** comfort

Questions for contemplation and discussion

1. The "Biographies of Exemplary Women" was intended as a guide-book for women. What character traits are being showcased in this story?

2. How would a modern person with feminist awareness assess the character of Yue Yangzi's wife?

3. Can you think of a sequel to this story about what happened to Yue Yangzi when he returned home after seven years?

4. Does the concept of "sacrificing life for righteousness" or "honor suicide" exist in other cultures of the world? Does it still exist today?

5. What do you think of the Western attitude that suicide is a sign of mental illness and is therefore something to be prevented at all costs?

Peace Consort Wang Zhaojun

For over two thousand years every Chinese emperor adopted a reign name when he ascended to the throne, and most of them also changed their reign names several times during their reign.[1] The reign names were intended to be auspicious, signifying the ambition and hope of the emperor. In the year 33 BCE, Emperor Yuan of the Han Dynasty adopted a fourth and last reign name of his sixteen-year reign: Jìngníng, meaning "peace at the border." Although he died of illness the same year, at the age of forty-two, he did live to see peace at the border. However, the credit for this accomplishment belongs to a heroine by the name of Wang Zhaojun.

When the Han Dynasty was founded in 202 BCE, a major challenge for the emperor was securing its northern border against the aggressive nomadic nations, mainly a group called the Xiongnu. Border conflict was a constant menace to the growing Han Empire.[2] Successive emperors managed it by a combination of diplomacy and military tactics. This situation persisted until about 51 BCE, when internal rivalry within the Xiongnu confederation split the nomadic nations into five chiefdoms, each led by a *shanyu*, meaning "chieftain." Huhanye, the *shanyu* closest to the Chinese border, was threatened by his more powerful older brother Zhizhi to the north. Huhanye decided to seek protection from his former foe the Han. The Han emperor, recognizing an opportunity

---

[1] This practice began with Emperor Wu of the Han Dynasty in 141 BCE and lasted until the end of the last dynasty—the Qing Dynasty— in 1911.

[2] The constant conflict was exacerbated by the Han Dynasty's own territorial expansion toward the north and west. Evidence of this can be seen in a timed map showing the continuous shifts in the territory under Han control. This is further corroborated by the segments of the Great Wall built during the Han Dynasty.

昭君出塞

在中国历代王朝两千多年的时间里，每一位皇帝在登基时都取一个年号，而多数的皇帝在其统治期间还数次更换年号[1]。年号寓意吉祥，代表着皇帝的志向和期望。公元前33年，汉元帝在其统治的十六年里第四次，也是最后一次，将年号更换为"竟宁"，即"边境安宁"。同年，汉元帝在42岁时驾崩，不过他确实看到了边境的安宁。然而，这一功劳应当归功于名叫王昭君的女英雄。

汉朝在公元前202年建立时，皇帝面对的一个很大挑战是如何应对北方边境上咄咄逼人的游牧民族，其中最主要的一支称为匈奴。边境冲突不断对日益强大的汉王朝是一种威胁[2]。历代皇帝都采取外交和军事策略相结合的方法加以应对。这种情形持续到公元前51年，当时匈奴联盟的内部纷争将其分裂为五个领地，由各自的单于统治。呼韩邪单于紧靠中国边境，而在他北边的哥哥郅支单于更加强悍，对呼韩邪造成了威胁。呼韩邪决定向之前的敌人汉朝廷寻求庇护。汉

---

[1] 皇帝取年号的做法始于公元前141年在位的汉武帝，一直延续到1911年最后一个王朝，即清朝末年。

[2] 汉朝向北和向西扩张其领土更加剧了持续不断的冲突。在一幅汉朝时期领土不断变化的定时地图上可以看到这方面的证据。汉代修建的长城分段也进一步证实了这一点。

to not only attain peace with this faction of the Xiongnu but also to drive a wedge between the two Xiongnu brothers, received Huhanye as an honored guest and showered him with lavish gifts.[3] After a month-long sojourn in the Han capital Chang'an, Huhanye was escorted home by a ten thousand-strong Han army, along with an enormous gift of grains for Huhanye's people.

---

[3] According to the *History of the Former Han*, these gifts consisted of 5 kg of gold, 200,000 cash coins, 77 suits of clothes, 8,000 bales of silk fabric, 1,500 kg of silk floss, and 15 horses.

朝皇帝意识到这不但是与这支匈奴取得和解的机会，而且可以借机扩大匈奴两兄弟之间的隔阂。因此，皇帝将来访的呼韩邪待为上宾，并赠送了厚礼[3]。呼韩邪在汉朝都城长安逗留了一个月之后，皇帝派一万大军护送他返回领地，并赠送了大批粮食给呼韩邪的百姓。

---

[3] 据《前汉书》记载，赠予呼韩邪的厚礼包括5公斤黄金、20万钱币、77套衣服、8000匹丝绸、1500公斤丝绵和15匹马。

In that same year, a girl by the name of Wang Zhaojun was born to a prominent family in a village on the north bank of the Yangtze River. She grew up to be an elegant young lady, cultivated in music and the arts. In her teens she was already well-known as the belle of her hometown, and in the year 36 BCE she was chosen to be a lady-in-waiting in the emperor's palace.

Three years later, in 33 BCE, the Xiongnu chieftain Huhanye made a second visit to the Han court to reinforce his alliance with the Han. This time, he proposed to enter into a "peace kinship" arrangement with Han China. That is, he asked Emperor Yuan for the hand of a princess in marriage, thus becoming a son-in-law to the Han emperor. Emperor Yuan was reluctant to marry off a daughter of his own to a foreign chieftain, so he chose one of his dispensable ladies-in-waiting and elevated her to the status of a princess before marrying her off to Huhanye. This lady turned out to be Wang Zhaojun.

On the day of the wedding, Emperor Yuan was stunned to find that Zhaojun was a dazzling beauty. Huhanye was delighted with the emperor's choice, even though he knew he was not given a true royal princess. The emperor immediately regretted his mistake, but it was too late for him to withdraw his promise to Huhanye. Before the wedding, the emperor had actually never laid eyes on Zhaojun. In those days, underlings of the emperor searched for beautiful ladies throughout the empire to be the emperor's "ladies-in-waiting." Most of these ladies spent the rest of their lives in the back palace, living a comfortable but lonely and boring life. Only a lucky few would be chosen by the emperor to become a wife or concubine, and the emperor made his choices based on the portraits painted by the court painter. The court painter aggrandized himself by extorting bribes from the ladies-in-waiting to make them look beautiful in the portraits. Out of self-respect and a moral sense, Zhaojun refused to bribe the court painter. As a result, the painter made her look homely, and even added an inauspicious birthmark

同年，名叫王昭君的女孩儿出生在长江北岸一个村子里的大户人家。她从小受音乐艺术的熏陶，成长为一名优雅的女子。昭君十几岁的时候，就已经是乡邻里人人皆知的美女了。公元前36年，昭君被选为了皇帝后宫的宫女。

　　三年后，即公元前33年，匈奴首领呼韩邪为了加强与汉朝廷的结盟，再次来到了长安。这次，他提出了希望与汉朝"和亲"的愿望，即请求汉元帝将一位公主许配给他，这样一来，他就是皇帝的女婿了。皇帝不愿意将自己的女儿远嫁到外国，于是就从后宫的宫女当中随便挑选一位，并册封为公主，再嫁给呼韩邪。这位被选中的宫女便是王昭君。

　　到了大婚的日子，汉元帝才惊讶地发现昭君原来是个绝色佳人。呼韩邪尽管知道嫁给他的并不是真正的公主，但对皇帝的选择万分满意。皇帝立刻感到后悔了，但要收回对呼韩邪的承诺已经太迟了。大婚之前，皇帝其实根本没见过昭君。那个年代，皇帝派人到各地去挑选美女，成为后宫的宫女。多数宫女就在后宫过着舒适又无聊的生活来度过余生。只有为数不多的几个幸运儿，会被皇帝选中成为皇后或妃子，而皇帝通常是看宫廷画师的画像来做选择。因此，宫廷画师总是趾高气扬，向宫女们索取贿赂，让她们在画像上看起来很漂亮。昭君是个自尊又有道德修养的女子，所以拒绝贿赂宫廷画师。于是，画师把昭君画得相貌平平，而且还在她的眼睛下面画了一颗黑痣，看上去不太吉利，这样就保证

below her eye, thus guaranteeing that she would never receive the emperor's favor. After Wang Zhaojun left Chang'an with Huhanye, the emperor launched a thorough investigation to find out why this dazzling beauty had never come to his attention. When the truth came out, the court painter was immediately executed.

Emperor Yuan's mistake in choosing Wang Zhaojun was partly his own fault. Rather than taking the trouble to personally screen the candidates, he asked an underling to find a volunteer from among the ladies-in-waiting. No sensible palace lady would want to be a concubine to a Xiongnu chieftain and emigrate to a harsh environment. The one exception was Wang Zhaojun. Having seen many aging ladies-in-waiting languish in the gilded cage of the back palace, she dreaded such a future for herself. Volunteering to be the "peace consort" was a way to escape her life of perpetual boredom and loneliness. What she did not realize was that she would become a national hero, forever revered by the Chinese people for sacrificing herself to bring goodwill and peace with a troublesome neighbor.

After Zhaojun moved to the land of the Xiongnu, she missed her motherland terribly, even though she was well-treated in her new home. When Huhanye died two years later, Zhaojun hoped that she could return to China, but she ended up following the Xiongnu custom of marrying the next chieftain, who happened to be Huhanye's oldest surviving son by his first wife (Zhaojun's stepson). When her second husband died nine years later, he was succeeded by a brother. This time, Zhaojun remained a widow until her death in 15 BCE at the age of thirty-six. She had a son and two daughters from her two husbands, who symbolized the union of two nations. To this day, she is memorialized for having brought half a century of stability to the Xiongnu and peace with China. Her mausoleum in Hohhot (capital of Inner Mongolia) remains a tourist destination today.

她永远不会得到皇帝的恩宠了。昭君跟着呼韩邪离开长安之后，皇帝下令彻查为何他从未注意到这位绝色佳人。真相大白之后，那个可恶的宫廷画师就被处决了。

汉元帝后悔莫及，但这多半应该归咎于他自己。他没有亲自过目候选人，而是派手下到后宫挑选一位毛遂自荐的宫女。除了王昭君，没有一个宫女愿意嫁给匈奴首领，移居到遥远又艰苦的地方。昭君看到一些年长的宫女在后宫这个金丝牢笼里渐渐老去，很害怕这就是她自己的未来。对她来说，自愿成为"和妃"是她挣脱枷锁，逃离无聊与孤独深渊的途径。她没想到自己的牺牲将为大汉王朝与昔日的宿敌换来亲善与和平，因而成为中国人民永远敬佩的民族英雄。

昭君移居到匈奴之后，尽管在那里受到厚待，但还是非常想念家乡。两年后，呼韩邪去世了。昭君当时希望返回长安，但最终还是按照匈奴的习俗嫁给了下一位首领，即呼韩邪与第一任妻子所生的长子，也就是昭君的继子。昭君的第二任丈夫在九年后也去世了，他的兄弟随后继位。这一次昭君没有再嫁，一直守寡到公元前15年去世，享年36岁。她与两任丈夫生育了一个儿子和两个女儿，成为了汉王朝与匈奴团结的象征。时至今日，人们因为昭君给汉王朝和匈奴带来了半个世纪和平稳定而纪念她。今天，位于呼和浩特（内蒙古自治区首府）的昭君墓仍然是一个旅游胜地。

Afterword

Wang Zhaojun became a legendary figure in Chinese culture soon after her death. Over the course of two millennia, poets, writers, dramatists, and even musicians have built an enormous cultural legacy around her. They include the greatest Tang poets Li Bai and Du Fu, down to twentieth-century writers like Cao Yu and Lao She. Yet, Wang Zhaojun was not unique as a "peace consort," nor was she the first. In fact, she was the last in a series of twelve Han "princesses" who were married to nomadic chieftains in the first half of the Han Dynasty. What made her case the ideal material for a Chinese "peace consort" legend was the power dynamics between the Han and the Xiongnu during her time.

Almost every emperor in the first half of the Han Dynasty (202 BCE–9 CE) had resorted to the "peace kinship" arrangement as a diplomatic strategy. But the purpose and outcome changed as the power dynamics between the Han court and the nomadic chiefdoms shifted. Nine of the twelve "peace kinship" arrangements were made with the Xiongnu, the nomads closest to the border with China.

This practice began around 200 BCE, just two years after the founding of the Han Dynasty. The powerful Xiongnu military leader Modu *shanyu* attacked China, and Emperor Gaozu personally led his forces to engage with him at Baideng Mountain, near present-day Datong. Gaozu's forces were besieged for seven days, and the emperor fled. The emperor, under duress and at the advice of his minister, made a peace treaty that included an annual tribute of Chinese luxury goods to the Xiongnu and a "peace kinship" arrangement that carried the possibility of Modu's successor being a half-Chinese grandson of the Han emperor. For almost a century the next six emperors followed this pattern of placating the aggressive Xiongnu through a combination of tribute and "peace kinship."

附 录

王昭君死后不久就成为了中国文化中的传奇人物。两千年来，诗人、作家、剧作家，甚至音乐家都围绕王昭君创作了大量的文学文艺作品，从唐朝最伟大的诗人李白和杜甫，到二十世纪的著名作家曹禺和老舍都是如此。然而，王昭君既不是史上唯一的"和妃"，也不是第一位。事实上，她是汉朝上半叶嫁给游牧首领的十二位"公主"中的最后一位。王昭君之所以成为中国"和妃"传奇的理想素材，正是因为她生活的时代反映了汉朝与匈奴之间的实力更迭。

汉朝的上半叶（公元前202年–公元9年），几乎每一位皇帝都将"和亲"作为一种外交策略。随着汉朝与游牧民族之间的实力更迭，和亲的目的和结果也随之发生了变化。在十二个"和亲"婚姻中，有九个是与最靠近中国边境的匈奴游牧民族缔结的。

和亲大约始于公元前200年，也就是汉朝建立仅两年后。强悍的匈奴冒顿单于进攻汉朝领地，汉高祖亲率大军在今天大同附近的白登山与之交战。高祖的军队被围困了七天七夜，皇帝也只好逃走了。无奈之下，高祖采纳了大臣的建议，承诺每年向匈奴进贡丰厚的奢侈品，并通过"和亲"的方式与匈奴缔结姻亲关系。如此一来，冒顿的继任者便有可能是有一半汉皇血统的孙子。在后来大约一百年的时间里，六位皇帝都采取了同样的方法，即进贡与"和亲"相结合来安抚强悍的匈奴。

It was during Emperor Wu's fifty-four-year reign (140–87 BCE) that the Han Dynasty reached the apex of its power. Three "peace kinships" were formed during his reign. The first, in 140 BCE, was along the same pattern as his predecessors. The latter two, in 108 BCE and 103 BCE, reflected a shift in regional power dynamics in favor of the Han. These two "princesses" were granted to the chieftain of Wusun, who sought alliance with the now powerful Han in order to combat the Xiongnu. This alliance was a win-win situation for Han and Wusun, and in fact gave Han the upper hand in the transaction. By 33 BCE, the year Wang Zhaojun was granted to Huhanye, the power shift was complete. In requesting the "peace kinship" arrangement, Huhanye in essence became a vassal to the Han court.

The diplomatic strategy of "peace kinship" was again deployed during the great Tang Dynasty (618–907 CE). More than ten Tang "peace consorts" were sent abroad in this era. The most celebrated case was between the founder of the Tibetan empire, King Songtsen Gampo, and the Chinese princess Wencheng, who also became a legendary hero.

In our modern-day world, the notion of arranging a marriage for diplomatic purposes may seem odd, perhaps even distasteful, but in ancient China it was considered the least costly way to buy temporary peace with a hostile nation or to forge an alliance against a common foe.

汉武帝在位的54年（公元前140年－公元前87年）是汉朝实力的巅峰期。他在位时有三次"和亲"。第一次发生在公元前140年，与之前的和亲方式相似。后两次分别发生在公元前108年和公元前103年。这两次和亲反映了区域实力开始向汉朝转移。这两次和亲的"公主"都被赐予了乌孙国的首领，而当时乌孙国为了对抗匈奴正在寻求与强大的汉朝结盟。这样的结盟对双方都有利，实际上使汉朝更占了上风。到了公元前33年，也就是王昭君被赐予呼韩邪的那一年，汉朝强大的实力已经形成了。呼韩邪请求"和亲"，本质上已经附属了汉朝廷。

"和亲"在大唐时期（618年－907年）再次被作为外交策略。这一时期唐朝送出的"和妃"有十多位，其中最著名的就是大唐的文成公主远嫁吐蕃帝国的开国君主松赞干布，而文成公主后来也成为了传奇英雄。

在当今的社会，以外交为目的的联姻也许会令人纳闷，甚至反感。然而，对古代中国皇朝来说，为了与敌国取得短暂的和平，或与一国结盟来对抗共同的敌国，"和亲"是以最低的代价获得最大利益的方法。

Vocabulary

1. 出塞 **chūsài** to go beyond the borders
2. 登基 **dēngjī** to be enthroned
3. 年号 **niánhào** reign name
4. 更换 **gēnghuàn** to change
5. 寓意吉祥 **yùyì jíxiáng** to impart an auspicious meaning
6. 志向 **zhìxiàng** aspiration
7. 驾崩 **jiàbēng** (emperor) to die
8. 归功于 **guīgōngyú** to attribute to, to give credit to
9. 应对 **yìngduì** to respond to
10. 咄咄逼人 **duōduō bīrén** aggressive
11. 游牧民族 **yóumù mínzú** nomadic tribes
12. 冲突 **chōngtū** conflict
13. 日益 **rìyì** increasingly
14. 威胁 **wēixié** to threaten; threat
15. 和···相结合 **hé ... xiāng jiéhé** to be combined with
16. 策略 **cèlüè** strategy
17. 联盟 **liánméng** alliance
18. 纷争 **fēnzhēng** dispute
19. 分裂 **fēnliè** to split
20. 单于 **chányú** chieftain (of a Xiongnu tribe)
21. 强悍 **qiánghàn** tough
22. 庇护 **bìhù** asylum, protection
23. 和解 **héjiě** reconciliation
24. 借机 **jièjī** to take advantage of an opportunity
25. 隔阂 **géhé** rift
26. 待为上宾 **dàiwéi shàngbīn** to treat as a guest of honor
27. 厚礼 **hòulǐ** generous gift
28. 逗留 **dòuliú** to stay
29. 大户人家 **dàhù rénjiā** prominent family
30. 受···熏陶 **shòu...xūntáo** to be influenced by (something positive)
31. 优雅 **yōuyǎ** graceful, elegant
32. 乡邻 **xiānglín** neighbors
33. 人人皆知 **rénrén jiēzhī** everyone knows
34. 结盟 **jiéméng** to form an alliance
35. 和亲 **héqīn** peace kinship
36. 许配 **xǔpèi** to betroth

37. 女婿 **nǚxù** son-in-law

38. 册封 **cèfēng** to confer a title (to someone)

39. 绝色佳人 **juésè jiārén** stunning beauty

40. 后悔 **hòuhuǐ** to regret

41. 承诺 **chéngnuò** promise

42. 度过余生 **dùguò yúshēng** to spend the rest of one's life

43. 为数不多 **wéishù bùduō** not many in number, few

44. 幸运儿 **xìngyùn'ér** the lucky one

45. 妃子 **fēizi** concubine

46. 趾高气扬 **zhǐgāo qìyáng** arrogant

47. 索取贿赂 **suǒqǔ huìlù** to extort bribes

48. 自尊 **zìzūn** self-respect

49. 道德修养 **dàodé xiūyǎng** moral cultivation

50. 相貌平平 **xiàngmào píngpíng** plain looking

51. 黑痣 **hēizhì** birth mark

52. 恩宠 **ēnchǒng** imperial favor

53. 彻查 **chèchá** to thoroughly investigate

54. 真相大白 **zhēnxiàng dàbái** the truth came out

55. 处决 **chǔjué** to execute

56. 后悔莫及 **hòuhuǐ mòjí** too late to regret

57. 归咎于 **guījiùyú** the blame goes to

58. 过目 **guòmù** to look over

59. 候选人 **hòuxuǎnrén** candidates

60. 毛遂自荐 **máosuì zìjiàn** to volunteer one's services

61. 移居 **yíjū** to emigrate

62. 金丝牢笼 **jīnsī láolóng** gilded cage

63. 和妃 **héfēi** peace consort

64. 挣脱枷锁 **zhèngtuō jiāsuǒ** to break free

65. 深渊 **shēnyuān** abyss

66. 途径 **tújìng** path

67. 昔日 **xīrì** former, in the old days

68. 宿敌 **sùdí** old enemy

69. 亲善 **qīnshàn** goodwill

70. 敬佩 **jìngpèi** to esteem, to admire

71. 厚待 **hòudài** to treat kindly and generously

72. 习俗 **xísú** custom

73. 长子 **zhǎngzǐ** eldest son

74. 继子 jìzǐ stepson

75. 继位 jìwèi to succeed (a position)

76. 守寡 shǒuguǎ to remain a widow

77. 享年 xiǎngnián to live a certain number of years

78. 象征 xiàngzhēng symbol; to symbolize

79. 首府 shǒufǔ capital

80. 墓 mù tomb

81. 旅游胜地 lǚyóu shèngdì tourist attraction

82. 传奇人物 chuánqí rénwù legendary person

83. 围绕 wéirào around; to surround

84. 既不是⋯也不是⋯ jì búshì... yě búshì... neither...nor...

85. 上半叶 shàngbànyè first half

86. 素材 sùcái material

87. 实力更迭 shílì gēngdié change in power dynamics

88. 外交策略 wàijiāo cèlüè diplomatic strategy

89. 缔结 dìjié to establish, to conclude (a treaty)

90. 亲率 qīnshuài to personally lead

91. 与之交战 yǔzhī jiāozhàn to engage in battle with them

92. 围困 wéikùn to be besieged

93. 无奈之下 wúnài zhīxià without any choice, under duress

94. 采纳 cǎinà to adopt (a suggestion)

95. 大臣 dàchén minister

96. 进贡 jìngòng to send tribute

97. 奢侈品 shēchǐpǐn luxury goods

98. 姻亲 yīnqīn relation by marriage, in-laws

99. 血统 xuètǒng lineage, blood line

100. 安抚 ānfǔ to appease

101. 巅峰 diānfēng peak

102. 区域实力 qūyù shílì regional power

103. 赐予 cìyǔ to bestow

104. 占⋯上风 zhàn...shàngfēng to have the upper hand

105. 附属 fùshǔ to be subordinate to, to be affiliated with

106. 吐蕃帝国 Tǔbō Dìguó Tibetan Empire

107. 君主 **jūnzhǔ** monarch

108. 联姻 **liányīn** marriage

109. 纳闷 **nàmèn** perplexed

110. 反感 **fǎngǎn** to be appalled

111. 短暂 **duǎnzàn** temporary

112. 代价 **dàijià** cost

fn1. 扩张 **kuòzhāng** to expand

fn2. 加剧 **jiājù** to exacerbate, to intensify

fn3. 持续不断 **chíxù búduàn** to continue without cease

fn4. 定时地图 **dìngshí dìtú** time map

fn5. 分段 **fēnduàn** segments

fn6. 赠予 **zèngyǔ** to give to

Questions for contemplation and discussion

1. Can you think of any instances in other parts of the world similar to the "peace kinship" described in this story?

2. Why do you think Wang Zhaojun has garnered such a large cultural legacy in China? Look up a literary work about her and tell a bit about it.

3. Has this story changed your previous impression of the Han Dynasty?

4. Another famous "peace consort" in Chinese history is Princess Wencheng 文成公主 from the Tang Dynasty. Research her story on the Internet or ask a Chinese friend about it. Then compare her story with that of Wang Zhaojun.

5. What do you think of "peace kinship" as a diplomatic ploy? How would you compare it with China's "panda diplomacy" in the late twentieth century?

An Emperor's Comfort Food

A proverb that has guided Chinese emperors through the ages is "the people are of supreme importance to a ruler, and food is of supreme importance to the people."[1] For most of Chinese history, the "people" meant the peasants who constituted the vast majority of the population. The advice embedded in this proverb is that a ruler must provide food security to the people, and failing to do so puts him in peril. No emperor understood this better than the founding emperor of the Ming Dynasty, Zhu Yuanzhang, for he was one of those peasants himself.

When the Mongol Kublai Khan first founded China's Yuan Dynasty in 1272, he ruled over the largest territory in China's history. But within half a century Yuan rule began to crumble. By the early fourteenth century natural disasters, famines, plagues, and peasant revolts increased. It was in 1328, during those turbulent times, that Zhu Yuanzhang was born. Zhu's parents were impoverished peasants in Anhui Province, an area traditionally known for its poverty. Zhu had many siblings, but most of them either died in early childhood or were given away because their parents could not afford to raise them. During a famine in 1344, when Zhu was sixteen, he witnessed both his parents and a brother die within a month of each other. He and his only surviving brother did not even have the means to give them a proper burial.

---

[1] This proverb was first spoken by Li Shiqi, an adviser to Liu Bang, the soon-to-be founder of the Han Dynasty in 204 BCE. Heeding this advice, Liu Bang defeated his rival Xiang Yu and became emperor. This is documented in *Historical Records* by Sima Qian.

珍珠翡翠白玉汤

中国的历代皇帝都将"王者以民为天，而民以食为天"[1]奉为圭臬。在中国的历史长河中，"民"指的就是占中国人口绝大多数的农民。这句名言包含着一个警示，即一位君王必须保证人民能吃饱饭，否则他会自身难保。最深谙这个道理的人可能就是明朝开国皇帝朱元璋，因为他本人也是农民出身。

在1272年元朝建立的时候，忽必烈统治着中国历史上最广大的疆域。但仅仅半个世纪以后，元朝的统治就开始分崩离析了。到了十四世纪初，天灾频发、饥荒遍地、瘟疫肆虐，再加上农民起义风起云涌。在那个兵荒马乱的年代，朱元璋于1328年出生在素以贫穷著称的安徽省的一个贫农家里。朱元璋有很多兄弟姐妹，但多半不是过早夭亡，就是由于贫困而让别人家领养去了。1344年又遇饥荒，十六岁的朱元璋亲眼目睹了自己的父母和大哥在一个月之内相继离世。他和唯一幸存的二哥连买棺材的钱都没有。

---

[1] 刘邦的谋士郦食其在公元前204年最早提出了这个说法。当时，刘邦即将成为汉朝的开国皇帝。据司马迁《史记》里的记载，刘邦在听取了郦食其的建议后，打败了项羽，成为了皇帝。

At this point Zhu sought refuge at a monastery, where he did menial work and begged for alms. But within a few weeks the monastery went bankrupt, and he became a wandering beggar. As a destitute vagabond, Zhu saw other parts of the country and learned a great deal about human nature—the good, the bad, and the ugly. After about three years he returned to the monastery. This time he studied Buddhism and acquired literacy from Buddhist monks. In 1352 the monastery was destroyed by the Yuan army on the pretext of suppressing a rebellion. Zhu was not a rebel at the time, but this event drove him to join one of the many rebel groups who were determined to overthrow the Yuan Dynasty. He rose quickly through the ranks, and eventually merged into the dominant Red Turbans forces, which ultimately led to the downfall of the dynasty. The final phase of overthrowing the Yuan Dynasty was complicated by rivalry among the rebel factions turned regional warlords. In 1356 Zhu conquered Nanjing and used it as his base of opera-

　　那时，无依无靠的朱元璋投奔到了一座寺庙里，靠着做一些粗活来填饱肚子。不料几个星期以后，寺庙就关门了，朱元璋便成了流落街头的乞丐。身为一个穷困的流浪汉，朱元璋浪迹天涯，对人性的善恶美丑有了深入的了解。三年后，他回到了寺庙，跟那里的僧人学佛，并习得了读写能力。1352年，元朝军队借口镇压叛乱摧毁了寺庙。朱元璋当时不是叛乱分子，但这起事件促使他加入了一支起义军，力图推翻元朝的统治。朱元璋在军队里晋升得很快，后来他的部队并入了势力强大的红巾军，最终推翻了元朝。由于各个起义军成为了不同的地方军阀，他们之间的相互争斗就使得元朝垮台的最后阶段变得十分复杂。1356年，朱元璋占领了

tion.[2] He was a brilliant military strategist, but it still took him another twelve years to subdue all the other warlords and drive the Yuan court out of China. In 1368, sixteen years after Zhu Yuanzhang first joined the rebel forces, he founded the Ming Dynasty and reigned for thirty years until his death in 1398.

Common folks in China had always yearned for a benevolent ruler who understood their lot and would care for them like a loving father. Zhu Yuanzhang's peasant roots and his downtrodden early life made him an ideal candidate for the role of a benevolent ruler. Having lost most of his family to famine, he certainly understood the proverb "food is of supreme importance to the people." This point is further bolstered by a pseudo-historical episode in Zhu's journey to the throne.

The story goes that after a battle where the rebel forces led by Zhu were defeated by Yuan forces, Zhu escaped by blending into the multitude of famine-stricken refugees. After days on the lam, he arrived at an abandoned temple, exhausted and famished. Soon two beggars who had been sheltering at the temple returned and found Zhu collapsed on the floor. They did what came naturally to them, which was to boil the food scraps they had managed to gather that day—a few clumps of burnt rice, some wilted spinach, and some rancid tofu. Then they roused the collapsed man and fed this soup to him. Revived by this life-saving concoction, Zhu asked his rescuers what it was. The two beggars had a habit of lifting their spirits by giving facetious names to whatever food scraps they could rustle up. On the spot they came up with euphemisms for the three ingredients—rice, spinach, and tofu— and called the concoction "pearls, jadeite, and white jade soup."

---

[2] Nanjing remained the capital of the Ming Dynasty until 1420, when the third emperor of the dynasty moved the capital to Beijing. Beijing had been the capital of the Yuan Dynasty, except it was called Dadu at the time. When the Mongol Dynasty was overthrown, it retreated to Xanada, which had been the capital of the Mongol Empire before it conquered China and remained the summer capital throughout the Yuan Dynasty.

南京，并将其作为自己的大本营。[2]朱元璋是一位杰出的军事家，但仍然用了十二年的时间才降服了各地的军阀，并将元朝廷赶出了中国地界。1368年，在揭竿起义十六年之后，朱元璋建立了明朝，成为了开国皇帝，统治大明王朝三十年，直到1398年去世。

中国的老百姓一直渴望有一位仁慈的明君，了解他们的疾苦，像慈父一样照顾他们。朱元璋出生于农民家庭，早年生活艰辛，使他成为了百姓心目中一位理想的仁君人选。朱元璋的多数家人都死于饥荒，他当然明白"民以食为天"这句名言。这一点在有关朱元璋起义时期的一则民间故事里也得到了证实。

相传，朱元璋率领的起义部队在一次战斗中被元军击败了，他混入一群逃难的饥民当中才得以脱险。东躲西藏了几天之后，他来到了一座废弃的寺庙，筋疲力尽又饥肠辘辘。不一会儿，借宿在这个寺庙里的两个乞丐回来了，发现朱元璋昏倒在了地上。两个乞丐像往常一样，将当天讨来的残羹剩饭煮了煮，有几块锅巴、一些蔫儿了的菠菜、还有几块馊豆腐。他们叫醒了朱元璋，给他喂了一些煮好的糊糊。喝了这碗救命的糊糊之后，朱元璋问他的救命恩人他喝的是什么。两个乞丐喜欢苦中作乐，常常给讨来的残羹剩饭取个美妙的名字。于是，他们俩灵机一动，告诉朱元璋他喝的米饭、菠菜和豆腐糊糊叫作"珍珠翡翠白玉汤"。

---

[2] 明朝建立后，定都南京，直到1420年第三任皇帝才将京城从南京迁往了北京。元朝一直将北京作为京城，不过那时候称北京为大都。元朝被推翻后，撤退至上都，也就是蒙古王朝征服中国以前的京城，后来一直作为元朝的夏都。

Twenty years later, after Zhu Yuanzhang had settled into his life as emperor, he grew bored with the sumptuous meals he was served and became lethargic. Remembering the "pearls, jadeite, and white jade soup" that had revived him twenty years earlier, he ordered the royal chef to make this soup. The soup produced by the royal chef turned out to be a huge disappointment to the emperor, so the poor chef was fired. The emperor then sent out a summons for the two beggars to come make this soup. This time, the emperor invited all his courtiers to partake of this energy-restoring comfort food. The two beggars made a big cauldron of the exact same soup that had revived the future emperor years earlier, but even before anyone tasted it the aroma made everyone nauseous. Undaunted, Zhu Yuanzhang immediately realized that it was the change in his own circumstances that made the same soup seem so different. In a moment of "remembering the bitter past and pondering the sweet present," he downed a bowl of this soup, then invited all the courtiers to join him. To the sycophant courtiers, an invitation from the emperor was an unchallengeable command, so every one of them took a big gulp of this soup. When the emperor asked them how they liked it, they were silent because they were still holding the soup in their mouths, waiting for an opportunity to spit it out. But all of them held up two thumbs to express their appraisal of the soup. The emperor pretended to take the two thumbs-up literally and ordered the two beggars to give each courtier two more bowls!

二十年后，朱元璋已经入主皇宫数年，开始厌倦宫廷里的山珍海味，经常没精打采。想起当年让他起死回生的"珍珠翡翠白玉汤"，朱元璋下令御厨烹制这道汤。结果，御厨做出来的根本不是当年的那个味儿，朱元璋大失所望，解雇了御厨。随后他颁布谕旨，传召那两个乞丐进宫，烹制珍珠翡翠白玉汤。这一次，皇上邀请了所有的大臣进宫，来品尝这道补气养生的美味汤。两个乞丐按照二十年前一模一样的方法，熬了一大锅当年救活未来皇上的珍珠翡翠白玉汤。这一次，大家还没品尝，飘出来的味儿已经让每个人都感到恶心。面不改色的皇上很快就意识到是自己的境遇改变了，汤才变了味儿。为了忆苦思甜，他端起汤碗一饮而尽，然后请众臣也效仿他喝了汤羹。对那些惯于阿谀奉承的大臣，皇上的旨意是不能违抗的，所以每个人都喝了一大口。皇上问大家汤的味道如何，没有一个人开口说话，因为大家嘴巴里的汤都还未下咽，含在嘴里等待时机吐出来。不过，人人都竖起两个大拇指，表示汤的味道好极了。皇上佯装不知真相，命令两个乞丐给每位大臣再添两碗汤！

Commentary

The above piece of pseudo-history is based on a popular comic cross-talk by Liu Baorui from the 1950s, during the early days of Communist China. It is only one of many stories of Zhu Yuanzhang being rescued from the brink of death by starvation, but it is unique in its political satire.

As for how well Zhu Yuanzhang measured up to the image of the benevolent ruler who understood the lot of the peasants, he definitely knew that "food is of supreme importance to the people," and that his own success hinged on providing a secure livelihood to the masses. To this end, he instituted agricultural reforms, promulgated new land policies, and resettled farmers in more favorable areas. But to put the Ming Dynasty on a secure footing, Zhu Yuanzhang had to restore normalcy to a nation ravaged by natural disasters, famines, plagues, and war. This he did accomplish in his thirty-year reign, but not without resorting to draconian measures which he implemented ruthlessly.

As for the "pearls, jadeite, and white jade soup," a much-improved version of it remains a comfort food to the Chinese people today. Nowadays, it is sometimes called by a more genuine name—"mixed leftovers soup."

评论

有关朱元璋在死亡边缘被拯救的故事有很多版本。以上的版本来自刘宝瑞在五十年代共产党执政初期创作的经典相声小品，具有其独特的政治讽刺意味。

至于朱元璋究竟在多大程度上符合体恤民情的仁君形象呢？他当然了解"民以食为天"，也明知自己的成功就在于让广大农民得以安居乐业。为此，朱元璋推行了农业改革，颁布了新的土地政策，并将农民重新安置在更宜于耕种居住的地区。但是，为了给明王朝打下牢固的基础，朱元璋必须让一个备受自然灾害、饥荒、瘟疫和战争蹂躏的国家恢复正常。朱元璋在其统治的三十年间，通过采取严厉的措施以及铁腕的手段的确实现了这一目标。

至于"珍珠翡翠白玉汤"，如今的改良版仍然深受中国人的喜爱，只不过人们有时候就把它叫做"剩菜杂合汤"，听起来更加名副其实了。

Vocabulary

1. 奉为圭臬 **fèngwéi guīniè** to honor (something) as the benchmark

2. 包含 **bāohán** to include

3. 警示 **jǐngshì** warning

4. 否则 **fǒuzé** otherwise

5. 自身难保 **zìshēn nánbǎo** unable to save themselves

6. 深谙 **shēn'ān** well versed in, to deeply understand

7. 开国皇帝 **kāiguó huángdì** founding emperor

8. 疆域 **jiāngyù** territory

9. 分崩离析 **fēnbēng líxī** to fall apart

10. 天灾频发 **tiānzāi pínfā** to have frequent natural disasters

11. 饥荒 **jīhuāng** famine

12. 瘟疫 **wēnyì** plague

13. 肆虐 **sìnüè** to rage

14. 起义 **qǐyì** uprising

15. 风起云涌 **fēngqǐ yúnyǒng** turbulent

16. 兵荒马乱 **bīnghuāng mǎluàn** turmoil and chaos of war

17. 素以···著称 **sùyǐ...zhùchēng** all along known for...

18. 贫农 **pínnóng** poor peasants

19. 夭亡 **yāowáng** to die prematurely

20. 目睹 **mùdǔ** to see with own eyes, to witness

21. 相继离世 **xiāngjì líshì** to pass away one after another

22. 幸存 **xìngcún** to survive (by luck)

23. 棺材 **guāncái** coffin

24. 投奔 **tóubèn** to seek refuge with...

25. 寺庙 **sìmiào** temple

26. 粗活 **cūhuó** menial work

27. 不料 **búliào** unexpectedly

28. 流落街头 **liúluò jiētóu** to roam on the street

29. 乞丐 **qǐgài** beggar

30. 穷困 **qióngkùn** destitute

31. 流浪汉 **liúlànghàn** tramp

32. 浪迹天涯 **làngjì tiānyá** to wander everywhere

33. 善恶美丑 **shànè měichǒu** good and evil, beauty and ugliness

34. 僧人 **sēngrén** monk

35. 镇压 **zhènyā** to suppress

36. 叛乱 **pànluàn** rebellion

37. 摧毁 **cuīhuǐ** to destroy

38. 促使 **cùshǐ** to spur, to impel

39. 力图 **lìtú** to try to...

40. 晋升 **jìnshēng** to advance (in rank)

41. 并入 **bìngrù** to merge into

42. 势力 **shìlì** power

43. 红巾军 **Hóngjīnjūn** Red Turban army

44. 军阀 **jūnfá** warlord

45. 垮台 **kuǎtái** to collapse

46. 占领 **zhànlǐng** to occupy

47. 大本营 **dàběnyíng** base camp

48. 杰出 **jiéchū** outstanding

49. 降服 **xiángfú** to subdue (also: to be subdued)

50. 地界 **dìjiè** boundary

51. 揭竿起义 **jiēgān qǐyì** to take up an uprising

52. 渴望 **kěwàng** to yearn for

53. 仁慈 **réncí** kind and compassionate

54. 明君 **míngjūn** enlightened ruler

55. 疾苦 **jíkǔ** suffering

56. 慈父 **cífù** loving father

57. 艰辛 **jiānxīn** full of hardship

58. 证实 **zhèngshí** confirmation; to confirm

59. 率领 **shuàilǐng** to lead

60. 脱险 **tuōxiǎn** to escape from dire straits

61. 东躲西藏 **dōngduǒ xīcáng** to hide here and there

62. 废弃 **fèiqì** abandoned

63. 筋疲力尽 **jīnpí lìjìn** utterly exhausted

64. 饥肠辘辘 **jīcháng lùlù** hungry (lit. hungry tummy rumbling)

65. 借宿 **jièsù** to stay for the night (lit. to borrow lodging)

66. 昏倒 **hūndǎo** to faint

67. 残羹剩饭 **cángēng shèngfàn** leftover soup and rice

68. 蔫儿 **niān'ér** to wilt

69. 馊豆腐 **sōu dòufu** rancid tofu

70. 糊糊 **húhu** mush

71. 救命恩人 **jiùmìng ēnrén** savior

72. 苦中作乐 **kǔzhōng zuòlè** to have fun amidst hardship

73. 灵机一动 **língjī yídòng** to have a flash of inspiration

74. 入主皇宫 **rùzhǔ huánggōng** to enter the imperial palace

75. 厌倦 **yànjuàn** to be bored with

76. 宫廷 **gōngtíng** palace

77. 山珍海味 **shānzhēn hǎiwèi** culinary delicacies

78. 起死回生 **qǐsǐ huíshēng** to rise from death and return to life

79. 下令 **xiàlìng** to send down an order

80. 御厨 **yùchú** royal chef

81. 烹制 **pēngzhì** to cook up

82. 解雇 **jiěgù** to fire, to dismiss

83. 颁布 **bānbù** to promulgate

84. 谕旨 **yùzhǐ** decree

85. 传召 **chuánzhào** to summon

86. 大臣 **dàchén** high officials

87. 品尝 **pǐncháng** to taste

88. 补气养生 **bǔqì yǎngshēng** (re: nutritious foods) to invigorate health

89. 熬 **áo** to simmer

90. 飘 **piāo** to float in the air

91. 恶心 **ěxin** nauseous

92. 面不改色 **miàn bù gǎisè** without changing facial expression

93. 境遇 **jìngyù** circumstances

94. 忆苦思甜 **yìkǔ sītián** to reminisce about bitterness (of the past) and think about sweetness (of the present)

95. 一饮而尽 **yìyǐn ér jìn** to drink up in one gulp

96. 效仿 **xiàofǎng** to mimic, to imitate

97. 阿谀奉承 **ēyú fèngchéng** to fawn on

98. 旨意 **zhǐyì** order, will

99. 违抗 **wéikàng** to defy

100. 下咽 **xiàyàn** to swallow

101. 竖起···大拇指 **shùqǐ ... dàmǔzhǐ** to do a thumbs up

102. 佯装 **yángzhuāng** to pretend

103. 真相 **zhēnxiàng** the truth

104. 拯救 **zhěngjiù** to save

105. 执政 **zhízhèng** to be in power

106. 经典 **jīngdiǎn** classic

107. 独特 **dútè** unique

108. 讽刺 **fěngcì** to satirize

109. 体恤民情 **tǐxù mínqíng** to empathize with the people

110. 安居乐业 **ānjū lèyè** to live and work in peace

III. 推行 **tuīxíng** to carry out

II2. 宜于 **yíyú** suitable for

II3. 牢固 **láogù** firm, durable

II4. 备受 **bèishòu** to suffer greatly

II5. 蹂躏 **róulìn** ravages, devastation

II6. 严厉 **yánlì** severe

II7. 措施 **cuòshī** measure, policy

II8. 铁腕 **tiěwàn** iron hand

II9. 改良版 **gǎiliángbǎn** improved version

I20. 名副其实 **míngfù qíshí** the name fits the real thing

fn1. 谋士 **móushì** advisor

fn2. 记载 **jìzǎi** to record; record

fn3. 迁往 **qiānwǎng** to move to

fn4. 撤退 **chètuì** to retreat

fn5. 征服 **zhēngfú** to conquer

Questions for contemplation and discussion

1. The grounds of the imperial palace that Zhu Yuanzhang built in Nanjing were very unusual in that they did not have flower gardens, but instead had only vegetable gardens. What does this tell us about Zhu Yuanzhang?

2. Dynastic change in China is always accompanied by a drastic reduction in population. In the eighteen years before the founding of the Ming Dynasty, it is estimated that China's population dropped by a third, from ninety million to sixty million. Can you explain why?

3. Among China's last five dynasties—the Tang, Song, Yuan, Ming, and Qing—the Yuan Dynasty lasted less than a century, much shorter than all the others. Can you think of some reasons for this?

4. The older generation in China today often admonish the younger generation with the proverb "remember the bitter past and ponder the sweet present." What do they mean by that?

5. What are some of your favorite comfort foods? Tell us why these foods are comforting to you.

Taming the New Year's Beast

Every culture in the world has its major holidays and each holiday has a story behind it. This folktale tells the story behind China's most important holiday, the Lunar New Year.

In ancient times there was a strange beast by the name of "Nián," which means "year." This beast had a huge unicorn jutting out from its forehead, sharp teeth, laser eyes that could pierce through one's heart, and spikes all over its body. This ferocious beast lived at the bottom of the ocean all year round, but on New Year's Eve it came on shore to gobble up domestic animals and attack people, especially children. Every

年兽的故事

世界上每一种文化都有自己主要的节日，而每个节日都有一个故事。这一章讲述的是中国最重要的节日，也就是农历新年的故事。

古时候，有一种名叫"年"的怪兽。它的额头上长着一只又长又尖的犄角，牙齿很锋利，凶狠的目光可以刺穿人的心脏，而且全身也长满了尖刺。这种怪兽常年生活在海底，但每年的除夕就会上岸来吞食家畜并伤害人们，尤其是小孩

year, on New Year's Eve, all the villagers ran into the mountains, supporting their frail elderly folks and carrying their children. They also locked up their domestic animals, hoping that Nián would not find them.

On the last day of a particular year, as the people of Peach Blossom Village were getting ready to evacuate to the mountains, an old beggar came into the village carrying a knapsack and a cane. He looked a little different from other beggars in that he had a long silvery beard, eyes that twinkled like stars, and a cheerful manner. Normally, the villagers would have been kind and generous to a beggar, but that day they were too busy packing, securing their animals in pens, gathering their families, and getting ready to run. No one paid any attention to the beggar until he reached the far end of the village where an old widow invited him into her cottage and offered him some dumplings. But she said, "I don't mean to rush you, but the Nián beast will be here after dark, so we must run and find a safe place in the mountains as soon as possible! So eat quickly!"

This bad news did not bother the old beggar one bit. "Oh, I know a thing or two about that monster," he chuckled as he picked up the first dumpling with his chopsticks. "You just go on to the mountains with the others, don't worry about me, I'll stay here and take care of that monster. But do you have a big piece of red cloth that I can borrow?"

The beggar's words made the old woman even more worried, but she did not have time to argue with him. She remembered the old red quilt that was part of her trousseau, so she pulled it out of a trunk and handed it to the beggar, saying, "I don't know what good this thing will do, but here it is. I've got to run. I hope you'll still be alive and well by the time I get back tomorrow."

Sure enough, Nián arrived at Peach Blossom Village right about midnight, but the village looked different from past years. Instead of being pitch dark, there was a cottage at the far end all lit up, as though a party was going on. "How wonderful," Nián thought to himself, "I can

子。因此，每年的除夕，村民们都扶老携幼逃进山里避难。人们也会把家里的牲畜都关起来，希望年兽找不到牠们。

有一年，除夕的这一天，桃花寨的村民们正忙着要往山里避难，村里来了一个老乞丐。他背着背包，挂着拐杖，看上去跟别的乞丐不一样。他留着银白色的长胡子，眼睛像星星一样闪闪发光，面色神清气朗。往常，村民们对乞丐总是热情慷慨，但那一天大家都忙着收拾东西、把牲畜圈起来、召集家人准备出逃。谁也没功夫理这个乞丐。乞丐走到村子的尽头，一个年老的寡妇才把他请进小屋里，煮了一些饺子给他吃。老寡妇接着说："我不想催你，不过天一黑年兽就要来了，所以我们得马上逃到山里，找个安全的地方躲起来。你快点吃吧！"

老乞丐听了寡妇的话并没有惊慌，反而抿嘴笑了笑，用筷子夹起一个饺子说："我对那个怪物略知一二，你快跟乡亲们去山里吧，别为我担心。我留下来对付那家伙。你有没有一块大红布可以借给我用一下？"

老寡妇听了乞丐的话更担心了，不过没时间跟他争辩了。她想起来自己的嫁妆里有一条旧的红被子，于是就从箱子里翻出来给了老乞丐，然后说："我不知道这东西有什么用，你拿去吧。我可得走了…但愿我明天回来的时候，你还活着。"

果然，年兽在半夜时分来到了桃花寨，但立刻感觉这次与往年有所不同。从前寨子里总是一片漆黑，今晚，寨子尽头的那个小屋灯火通明，屋里好像很热闹。"太好了，"年兽自言自语地说，"这回我一下子就能抓到好几个！"年兽走到

catch a bunch of people all at once!" As he neared the door, he saw red slips of paper taped all around the frame. As he stepped closer to investigate, the door swung open. Immediately there was an outburst of sparks, followed by a barrage of explosions. The next thing Nián saw was a monster draped in a red cape laughing as he came after him. Nián turned around and ran for his dear life. As it turned out, there were three things that Nián was afraid of: sparks, explosive sounds, and the color red. But up to this point, only the old beggar knew this.

When the villagers returned the next morning, they expected to find their village devastated and perhaps some chickens and sheep gone. But they were surprised that all was peaceful and quiet and everything was just as they had left it the night before. At that moment the old widow realized that the old beggar must have had something to do with this. "Follow me," she said to the others, "we'll find out what happened." In front of her cottage was a pile of burned-out red firecrackers, her door frame was decorated with auspicious New Year sayings written on red strips of paper, and inside the cottage several red candles were still burning on the kitchen table. The old beggar was nowhere to be found, but there was no doubt in the old widow's mind that this was all his doing. She congratulated herself for having invited him in when she herself was frantically getting ready to leave the previous night. Having gotten through the night unharmed by the Nián beast, the villagers were so relieved that they went around hugging each other.

From then on all the villagers knew what they must do every New Year's Eve to ward off Nián's attack: hang red slips of paper with auspicious sayings around their doors, set off firecrackers, and stay up all night in a room lit up by red candles. They also taught folks in nearby villages to do the same. That is how all these New Year's customs gradually spread throughout China.

小屋面前，看见门框上贴了红对联。牠刚走近一点，想看个究竟的时候，门突然敞开了。刹那间，火花四溅，紧跟着一阵噼噼啪啪的爆炸声。随后，年兽看见一只身披大红斗篷的怪物大笑着朝牠奔来。年兽大惊，赶紧掉头逃窜。原来，年兽最怕三样东西：火光、爆炸声和红色。但那个时候，只有老乞丐知道这个秘密。

第二天早上，村民们回来时，以为会看见村子里一片狼藉，或许会少了一些鸡和羊。没想到，村子里一片祥和宁静，一切都跟他们前一晚离开时一模一样。那一刻，老寡妇恍然大悟，心想肯定是那个老乞丐的功劳。她告诉乡亲们："大家跟我来，看看到底是怎么一回事儿。"在她的小屋门前，大家看到一堆鞭炮屑，门框上贴满了写着新年祝福的红对联，屋里的饭桌上还点着几支红蜡烛。老乞丐已经不见了，但老寡妇心里明白，所有这一切都是老乞丐干的。她很庆幸自己在前一天晚上要急忙离开的时候把他请进了家里。村民们安然躲过了除夕夜，都松了一口气，相拥同庆。

从此以后，村民们都知道每年的除夕夜必须要做哪些事情来抵御年兽了：门上要贴写着新年祝福的红对联，燃放鞭炮，在点着红蜡烛的房间里守岁。村民们也把这些做法传授给邻近的村子。久而久之，过年的习俗就在中国各地传开了。

Afterword

It may seem strange that the story behind China's most important holiday is about a monster. Why is it not something more jolly, like the Santa Claus story in the West? Children in every culture love stories about monsters and how they are vanquished in the end. But why did it become the theme for the Lunar New Year holiday? We have some inkling of this puzzle in two Chinese words.

The most often used Chinese word for "celebrating new year" is "*guònián*, passing from one year to the next," but this word is a short form of the term "*guò niánguān*, passing through the critical juncture between the old and new year." The key difference lies in the word "*guān*," which implies a dangerous hurdle that one might or might not pass.

The word for New Year's Eve is "*chúxī*, eliminate ... at sunset." The thing that is being eliminated is unstated in this word, but we have a clue from the classical text *Master Lü's Spring and Autumn Annals* (ca. 239 BCE), as follows: "On the day before the new year, our ancestors held a 'big exorcism' ritual, using drums to drive away the epidemic demons."

Putting the two words "*chúxī*" and "*guò niánguān*" together, we surmise that Chinese ancestors saw the demons as a hurdle that needed to be eliminated before they could pass safely to the new year. It was also their hope that in the new year they would not be plagued by these demons.

Life in ancient times was precarious and unpredictable. People had no control over droughts, floods, pestilence, and other disasters, so they attributed these disasters to the spirit world. To protect themselves from these disasters, they created rituals to placate or eliminate the evil spirits. Thus, the story of the New Year's beast is an allegory about eliminating sinister forces from their lives. This interpretation is bolstered

附 录

中国最重要的节日怎么会跟一种怪兽联系在一起呢？这似乎很奇怪。为什么不是一个像西方圣诞老人一样欢乐的故事呢？世界各国的儿童都喜爱鬼怪故事，也很高兴看到鬼怪最终没有好下场。可是怪兽为什么变成了农历新年的主题呢？中文里的两个词或许可以帮助我们解开这个谜。

中文里"庆祝新年"最常用的词是"过年"，即从一年过到下一年。其实，"过年"是"过年关"的缩写，意思是度过旧年与新年交替的紧要关头。"过年"与"过年关"的重要差别在于"关"这个字，指的是一个危险的关口，而一个人有可能过得去，也有可能过不去。

"新年前夜"在中文里称为"除夕"，是"在日落的时候消除…"的意思。被消除的东西没有明说，不过我们从古书《吕氏春秋》（约公元前239年）中可以得到一些线索："古人在新年的前一天举行"大傩"仪式，用击鼓的方式来驱逐"疫病之鬼。"

把"除夕"和"过年关"这两个词放在一起，我们推测中国人的祖先相信，只有在新年前消除恶魔才能够平安过年。同时，他们也希望在新的一年里不会被恶魔侵扰。

古代的生活朝不保夕又变幻莫测。人们在旱灾、涝灾和瘟疫等灾害面前束手无策，因此，只能将这些灾害归咎于神灵的世界。为了保护自己免受灾害的影响，人们创造了各种仪式来安抚神灵或消除恶魔。简言之，年兽的故事就是一个消除人们生活中邪恶势力的寓言故事。这个推测有事实的依

by the fact that the name Nián ("year") is given to this beast who used to ravage people every New Year's Eve.

In modern times, the notion of "eliminating evil forces" and "getting through the monster hurdle" no longer has practical reality. Lunar New Year has become an extended, joyful holiday, celebrated by family reunions, feasts, new clothes, and money in red envelopes. But the "evil spirit" still lurks around people living in poverty or loneliness during this time. These people take no part in the joys of the holiday and may still be plagued by poverty and illness. In addition, there is the custom of paying one's debts before the New Year. Those who are in debt will often skip town to avoid the demon in the form of the creditor coming after them.

The story of the New Year's beast continues to be passed down from generation to generation. Perhaps this is a reminder that poor people are still plagued by Nián, and for their sake we need to eliminate this beast, even as we celebrate the holiday ourselves.

据，即"年"这个名字被赋予了曾经在每年的除夕夜出来蹂躏百姓的怪兽。

如今，"消除恶势力"与"闯过恶魔关"的说法不再有实际意义了。农历新年已经成为了亲人团聚、共享美味佳肴、穿新衣、发红包的一个喜庆节日。但"妖魔鬼怪"在这段时间里仍然潜藏在贫困或孤独的人们身边。他们无法享受节日的欢乐，可能仍受到贫困和病痛的侵扰。此外，过年也有年底必须还清债务的习俗。那些欠债的人往往会远离家乡，以躲避追债的恶魔债主。

时至今日，年兽的故事依然代代相传。这提醒我们贫穷的人们仍然受到"年"的侵扰。我们自己在欢度农历新年的同时，也必须为不幸的他人消除年兽。

Vocabulary

1. 讲述 **jiǎngshù** to tell, to narrate
2. 农历 **nónglì** lunar calendar
3. 怪兽 **guàishòu** strange beast
4. 额头 **étóu** forehead
5. 犄角 **jījiǎo** horn
6. 锋利 **fēnglì** sharp
7. 凶狠 **xiōnghěn** fierce
8. 刺穿 **cìchuān** to pierce
9. 尖刺 **jiāncì** sharp spike
10. 除夕 **chúxī** Lunar New Year's Eve
11. 吞食 **tūnshí** to devour
12. 家畜 **jiāxù** domestic animals
13. 扶老携幼 **fúlǎo xiéyòu** to support the old and carry the young
14. 避难 **bìnàn** to flee from disaster, to seek refuge
15. 牲畜 **shēngxù** livestock
16. 桃花寨 **Táohuāzhài** Peach Blossom Village
17. 乞丐 **qǐgài** beggar
18. 拄… **zhǔ…** to lean on (a stick)
19. 拐杖 **guǎizhàng** cane
20. 神清气朗 **shénqīng qìlǎng** to

have a clear and bright spirit

21. 热情慷慨 **rèqíng kāngkǎi** warm and generous
22. 召集 **zhàojí** to gather up (people)
23. 尽头 **jìntóu** the end
24. 寡妇 **guǎfù** widow
25. 催 **cuī** to rush (someone)
26. 躲起来 **duǒqǐlái** to hide
27. 惊慌 **jīnghuāng** to panic
28. 抿嘴 **mǐnzuǐ** to purse the lips
29. 略知一二 **lüèzhī yī'èr** to know a thing or two
30. 对付 **duìfu** to deal with
31. 争辩 **zhēngbiàn** to argue
32. 嫁妆 **jiàzhuāng** trousseau
33. 被子 **bèizi** quilt
34. 半夜时分 **bànyè shífēn** the hour of midnight
35. 漆黑 **qīhēi** pitch black
36. 灯火通明 **dēnghuǒ tōngmíng** brightly lit
37. 门框 **ménkuàng** door frame
38. 对联 **duìlián** couplet

39. 看个究竟 **kànge jiūjìng** to check it out

40. 刹那间 **chànàjiān** in an instant

41. 火花四溅 **huǒhuā sìjiàn** sparks flying

42. 噼噼啪啪 **pīpīpāpā** crackling sound (onomatopoeia)

43. 爆炸声 **bàozhà shēng** explosive sound

44. 身披 **shēnpī** to drape over the body

45. 斗篷 **dǒupéng** cloak

46. 奔 **bēn** to run

47. 掉头逃窜 **diàotóu táocuàn** to turn around and flee

48. 秘密 **mìmì** secret

49. 一片狼藉 **yípiàn lángjí** in total disarray

50. 祥和宁静 **xiánghé níngjìng** peaceful and tranquil

51. 恍然大悟 **huǎngrán dàwù** to suddenly realize

52. 功劳 **gōngláo** credit

53. 鞭炮屑 **biānpàoxiè** firecracker shreds

54. 祝福 **zhùfú** to bless; blessings

55. 蜡烛 **làzhú** candle

56. 庆幸 **qìngxìng** to rejoice

57. 安然 **ānrán** safely

58. 松了一口气 **sōngle yìkǒuqì** to be relieved

59. 相拥同庆 **xiāngyōng tóngqìng** to hug each other and celebrate

60. 抵御 **dǐyù** to fend against

61. 燃放 **ránfàng** to set off (firecrackers)

62. 守岁 **shǒusuì** to stay up on New Year's Eve

63. 传授 **chuánshòu** to transmit (knowledge)

64. 久而久之 **jiǔ ér jiǔ zhī** over time

65. 鬼怪 **guǐguài** ghost

66. 下场 **xiàchǎng** ending, consequence

67. 解开···谜 **jiěkāi...mí** to solve the riddle

68. 缩写 **suōxiě** abbreviation

69. 度过 **dùguò** to pass through

70. 交替 **jiāotì** to replace, to switch from one to the other

71. 紧要关头 **jǐnyào guāntóu** critical juncture

72. 关口 **guānkǒu** a pass, check point

73. 消除 **xiāochú** to eliminate

74. 线索 **xiànsuǒ** clue

75. 大傩 **dànuó** big exorcise

76. 击鼓 **jīgǔ** to beat a drum

77. 驱逐 **qūzhú** to drive away

78. 疫疬之鬼 **yìlì zhī guǐ** the plague demon

79. 推测 **tuīcè** to surmise

80. 恶魔 **èmó** demon

81. 侵扰 **qīnrǎo** to harass

82. 朝不保夕 **zhāo bùbǎo xī** precarious (lit. in the morning, there's no guarantee about the evening)

83. 变幻莫测 **biànhuàn mòcè** unpredictable

84. 旱灾 **hànzāi** drought

85. 涝灾 **làozāi** flood

86. 瘟疫 **wēnyì** plague

87. 束手无策 **shùshǒu wúcè** helpless, at wit's end

88. 归咎于 **guījiùyú** to place blame on

89. 神灵 **shénlíng** the spirits

90. 免受 **miǎnshòu** to be spared (something evil)

91. 仪式 **yíshì** rituals

92. 安抚 **ānfǔ** to appease

93. 简言之 **jiǎnyánzhī** in short, simply put

94. 邪恶势力 **xié'è shìlì** evil forces

95. 寓言 **yùyán** fable

96. 依据 **yījù** basis; according to

97. 赋予 **fùyǔ** to bestow on

98. 蹂躏 **róulìn** to ravage

99. 闯过 **chuǎngguò** to break through

100. 美味佳肴 **měiwèi jiāyáo** delicious foods

101. 妖魔鬼怪 **yāomó guǐguài** demons and ghosts

102. 潜藏 **qiáncáng** to lurk beneath the surface

103. 孤独 **gūdú** lonely

104. 还清债务 **huánqīng zhàiwù** to pay up all the debts

105. 欠债 **qiànzhài** to be in debt

106. 躲避 **duǒbì** to dodge

107. 追债 **zhuīzhài** to collect debt

108. 债主 **zhàizhǔ** creditor

109. 代代相传 **dàidài xiāngchuán** to pass down from generation to generation

Questions for contemplation and discussion

1. Did you learn anything new from this story about the Chinese Lunar New Year that you didn't know before?

2. The two heroes in the New Year's beast story are the beggar and the old widow. Why do you think these two figures were chosen for these heroic roles?

3. In this story the villagers never actually saw Nián, and except for the old widow neither did they have contact with the old beggar. Why do you think the storyteller made it so?

4. Can you recall a monster story from your childhood? Tell what you like or dislike about this story.

5. In modern times many traditional holidays in China and the West have become commercialized. How do you feel about this?

China's Romeo and Juliet

During the Eastern Jin Dynasty (317–420)[1], in Shangyu County, Kuaiji Prefecture, there was a local official named Master Zhu, who had a daughter named Yingtai. While this family raised their daughter to be a proper young lady of the times, she grew up with several older brothers and was allowed to study poetry and literature with them. She especially admired the historical and literary works of two eminent women writers of the Han Dynasty—Ban Zhao and Cai Wenji—and saw them as role models for herself. When she became a teenager, she longed to become a serious scholar, but there were no qualified teachers near her hometown. She begged her father to let her go study at the Wansong Academy in Hangzhou, and of course he refused. Not one to give up easily, she dressed herself up as an itinerant fortune-teller and went to her father to plead again, saying "According to my divination, it would be best to let your beloved daughter go to Hangzhou." Master Zhu could not bear to disappoint his daughter, and she did indeed look and sound like a young man, so he reluctantly agreed. But he ordered Yingtai's handmaiden to also dress up like a young man to accompany her. Before the pair left home, Master Chu also made Yingtai promise to return home after three years, when she would have reached the proper age to be married.

---

[1] Between the two great dynasties of Han and Tang, China went through a period of disunion that lasted almost four centuries. As one of the Six Dynasties, Eastern Jin occupied a large territory that included the major cultural centers. It was politically unstable and disunified, but was notable for its cultural achievements.

梁山伯与祝英台

东晋时期（317年－420年）[1]，会稽郡上虞县的祝员外家里有一个女儿，名叫英台。英台从小就接受传统大家闺秀的家庭教育，但她跟几个哥哥一起长大，于是家里也让她跟哥哥们一起习读诗书。英台特别欣赏汉代两位著名女作家班昭和蔡文姬的历史文学作品，并视她们为自己的偶像。花季年龄的英台渴望成为一名学者，但家附近没有称职的老师。她乞求父亲让她去杭州的万松书院读书，父亲当然不允。英台不甘心，乔装打扮成游走的算命先生，又去找父亲求情。她说："照卦来看，最好让令爱去杭州求学。"祝员外不忍心让女儿失望，再说，她女扮男装的面相和声音都是一个标准的年轻小生，于是父亲很不情愿地答应了。不过，他吩咐英台的侍女也扮成书童，陪伴在女儿身边。英台和侍女离家前，父亲让英台保证三年后回到家中，那时她也到了出嫁的年龄了。

---

[1] 在汉唐两大盛世王朝之间，中国经历了将近四个世纪的分裂时期。作为六朝之一的东晋，其领土面积包括了主要的文化中心。东晋在政治上不稳定，也不统一，但在文化上成就卓著。

Not long after Yingtai and her companion had set out on their journey, they met a young man, Liang Shanbo, from another county headed to the same academy in Hangzhou. The two young scholars hit it off so well that they became sworn brothers even before they arrived in Hangzhou. They ended up studying and living together as brothers, even sharing a bed, as was common in those days. As you can imagine, Yingtai soon fell in love with Shanbo, while Shanbo became a big brother to Yingtai.

In the third year of their studies, Yingtai grew increasingly anxious about leaving Shanbo, and began wishing they could be soulmates for

　　英台和侍女上路不久，就遇见了来自另外一个县的青年梁山伯，也去杭州万松书院读书。两个年轻人相见恨晚，还没到杭州就结下金兰之好。到了杭州以后，两人同窗共读，情同手足，甚至同床共眠。可想而知，英台很快就爱上了山伯，而山伯只把英台看作自己的亲弟弟。

　　读书的第三年，英台开始担心不久就要离开山伯了。尽管她知道山伯的家境比不上自己的，但心里仍希望可以与他

life, even knowing that Shanbo's family could not match hers in terms of status and wealth. On several occasions she gave Shanbo hints of her true gender, but he was simply too dense to get the hints. On one occasion he even teased her for acting like a girl, but it was inconceivable to him that this "brother" with whom he had shared his life for three years was a girl in disguise.

At the end of three years, when Master Zhu wrote to Yingtai urging her to come home, she had no choice but to obey him as promised. But she made a secret plan to bring Shanbo to meet her family and propose marriage. She told him that she had a sister of marriageable age and suggested that he come to ask her father Master Zhu for the hand of this sister. Shanbo was delighted with this plan because he would then become Yingtai's brother-in-law, thus guaranteeing that they would remain close forever. However, Shanbo came from a poor family and needed time to assemble a respectable proposal gift. Meanwhile, before Yingtai's plan could unfold, her father Master Zhu had already betrothed her to Ma Wencai, the son of an eminent and wealthy official. In doing so, Master Zhu thought he had done very well by his beloved daughter.

By the time Shanbo arrived in Shangyu and saw Yingtai as her true self, it was already too late. The reunion at which Yingtai had hoped to be engaged to Shanbo turned out to be their final farewell. The two shed tears as they pledged their undying love for each other. Together they vowed that if they could not be together in this life, they would reunite after death.

Shortly after they parted, Liang Shanbo received an imperial appointment as county magistrate. However, this great honor did not lift him out of his despair from losing Yingtai and he died of a broken heart not long after taking office. His family, following his final wishes, buried him in a grave near Yingtai's hometown.

永结同心、白头偕老。有好几次，英台暗示山伯她实际上是女儿身，但山伯根本没反应过来。有一次，他甚至调侃她的举止像个女孩子。当然，山伯无论如何也想不到这个与他朝夕相处三年的"弟弟"竟然是女扮男装的大家闺秀。

到了第三年底，祝员外写信给英台，催她赶紧回家。英台只能信守承诺，准备返回家中。不过她心生一计，要山伯来见她的家人并提亲。她告诉山伯自己有一个妹妹，已经到了出嫁的年龄，山伯应该来她家向父亲提亲。山伯听了很高兴，这样一来，他就成了英台的妹夫，两人可以一辈子都在一起。然而，山伯家境贫寒，准备一份体面的聘礼要花一段时间。没想到，英台的计划还没实现，她的父亲已经将她许配给了当地名门望族的儿子马文才。在祝员外看来，他为心爱的女儿安排了一门很好的亲事。

等山伯到了上虞，见到大家闺秀英台时，一切都已经晚了。英台原来期盼与山伯的重逢之日，便是他们二人订婚的喜庆之时。没想到，这一天竟成了他们永别的日子。两人伤心欲绝，泪流满面，誓言他们的爱至死不渝，生不能同衾，死也要同穴。

两人分别后不久，梁山伯就被朝廷任命为县令。然而，晋升官职的荣耀也没能将山伯从失去英台的悲痛中解脱出来，上任不久就伤心离世了。家人遵照山伯的遗愿，将他葬在了英台家乡附近的一座坟墓里。

Soon it was time for Yingtai to be escorted to her wedding with Ma Wencai. On the way to the Ma family's hometown, just as the wedding entourage came near Liang Shanbo's gravesite, a thunderstorm started, forcing the entourage to pause and wait for it to blow over. Suddenly there was a flash of lightning, immediately followed by an ear-splitting clap of thunder. Everyone in the wedding entourage ran for cover except Yingtai. She was the only one who saw Shanbo's grave split open by the lightning and she quickly leaped into the chasm. Soon the storm blew over, a rainbow appeared on the horizon, and the grave closed. Yingtai was nowhere to be found. The wedding entourage only saw two butterflies circling each other above the grave. The butterflies lingered there long after the wedding entourage had given up searching for Yingtai and departed.

Afterword

The above story is purported to be based on historical reality, although obviously it has acquired some fictional elements. One would naturally wonder how Yingtai could have disguised herself as a man and go undetected for three years. On this question, numerous answers can be found by googling "古代女扮男装 (women disguised as men in ancient times)" on the Chinese Internet. What we know for sure is that Chinese history has documented numerous cases of women disguising themselves as men in order to be scholars, officials, or warriors, all roles that were historically denied to women. We have no way to know about the cases that were never discovered. What we can offer here are some cases that were exposed.

很快就到了英台嫁给马文才的大喜日子。在送亲的花轿抬着英台去马家的路上，刚走到梁山伯坟墓的附近，突然来了一场暴风雨。送亲的队伍只好停下来躲避雷雨。突然，一道闪电划过，紧接着一声震耳欲聋的炸雷滚滚而来。送亲的人纷纷躲避，只有英台一个人看见山伯的坟墓在电闪雷鸣中裂开了。她纵身一跃，跳进了坟墓。暴风雨很快过去了，天边出现了一道彩虹，坟墓的裂缝又合上了，英台也不见了。送亲的人们看见两只蝴蝶在坟墓上空翩翩起舞。大家找不到英台，最终离开之后，两只蝴蝶还久久不肯离去。

附 录

梁祝的故事据称取材于史实，但显然加入了虚构的成分。有人自然会问，英台怎么可能女扮男装三年都没被发现呢？就这个问题，在中国的互联网上搜索"古代女扮男装"便可以找到众多的答案。我们很清楚的一点是，中国历史记载的女扮男装成为学者、官员和战士的例子数不胜数，而女性在历史上也只有女扮男装才有可能担当这些角色。女扮男装没被发现的案例，我们当然无从知晓。但我们可以看看以下被发现的案例。

Lou Cheng of the Southern Qi Dynasty (479–502): She circulated among elite scholars and was best known as a champion in the boardgame of *Go*. She became an official in Yangzhou by way of recommendation. When she was discovered, she resigned her post and returned home. The emperor expressed his regrets but did not retain her.

Madam Meng (ca. 805) of the Tang Dynasty: Her husband Zhang Cha was a military official on the northern frontier. When he died, she disguised herself as his younger brother and took over his position in the military. When she was discovered, she was officially appointed to the position that she had *de facto* undertaken.

Huang Chonggu of the Five Dynasties period (907–960): She traveled widely, circulated among scholars, and became an official by recommendation. The governor was so impressed by her abilities and dignified manner that he offered his own daughter in marriage. Overwhelmed by this favor that she could not accept, she sent the governor a confession in the form of a poem. In the end, she left her post and returned home with a generous stipend.

Zhang Yujing (ca. 1400) of the Ming Dynasty: From early childhood, she excelled in martial arts and became a leader in her home village. When she went to the capital to compete in the imperial military exam, she was discovered. By law she could have been executed, but the emperor, out of curiosity, gave her an audience. He was so impressed with her that he granted her the title "female valedictorian" and commissioned her to be a martial arts teacher in the imperial palace.

The most renowned case in China as well as the West is that of Hua Mulan. During the Northern Wei Dynasty (386–535), when China was harassed by the nomadic tribes from Mongolia, every family that received a draft summons had to send an able-bodied man. The father in the Hua family was too old and the only son was underage, so Mulan decided to answer the draft disguised as a man. She fought alongside her male comrades for twelve years and was never detected. As a reward

南齐（479年－502年）的娄逞：凭借下得一手好围棋，娄逞结交了一群文人墨客。经友人举荐娄逞到扬州做了官员。后来，她被发现是女儿身，便辞官回乡了。皇帝觉得很可惜，但并没有挽留她。

唐朝的孟夫人（约805年）：她的丈夫张詧曾是朔方兵马使。丈夫去世后，孟夫人假扮成丈夫的弟弟，接替丈夫在军中的职位。身份暴露之后，孟夫人被正式任命为了朔方兵马使。

五代时期（907年－960年）的黄崇嘏：她游历四方，结交文人墨客，被举荐成为官员。知州很欣赏她的才华，想招为女婿。她受宠若惊，又无法接受，于是给知州写了一首诗，坦言了自己的性别。随后，她辞了官职，得到一笔丰厚的俸禄，返回了家乡。

明朝的张玉景（约1400年）：从小就擅长武术，成为了乡里的武术队长。在进京参加宫廷比武选拔时，被发现原来是女子。因为犯了欺君之罪，她本来应被斩首。但皇帝很好奇，召见了张玉景。她在黄帝面前临死不惧，慷慨陈词，皇帝欣赏她的勇气，赐予了她"女状元"的称号，并任命她为宫廷武术教官。

在海内外最著名的例子要数花木兰了。北魏时期（386年－535年）北方蒙古游牧部落不断地侵扰中国，接到招兵命令的每户人家都必须派出一名壮丁。花家的父亲年事已高，唯一的儿子还未成年，因此，木兰决定女扮男装应征入伍。她与男战士们并肩作战十二年，从未被发现是女儿身。

for her distinguished leadership, the emperor appointed her as a general. However, she declined on the grounds that her aging parents needed her care. A group of comrades who were reluctant to part with her escorted her home. It was then that she retreated into a backroom and came out dressed as her female self, much to the astonishment and amusement of her comrades.

The story of the "butterfly lovers" and the legend of Mulan are all-time favorites in China. They have appeared in various literary and theatrical forms through the ages. From this, we surmise that beneath the overt restrictions on women in traditional Chinese culture, there has all along been an undercurrent of "feminist consciousness," the recognition that women are capable of everything that men are. The tragedy of the "butterfly lovers" can also be seen as a quiet protest against societal norms, and a testimony to the yearning of men and women to have a true soulmate for life.

Vocabulary

1. 员外 **yuánwài** squire

2. 大家闺秀 **dàjiā guīxiù** genteel lady from prominent family

3. 习读诗书 **xídú shīshū** to study literature and poetry

4. 欣赏 **xīnshǎng** to appreciate

5. 视…为… **shì…wéi…** to regard…as…

6. 偶像 **ǒuxiàng** idol

7. 花季 **huājì** (girls) teenage (lit. flowering season)

8. 渴望 **kěwàng** to yearn for

9. 称职 **chènzhí** competent, qualified

10. 乞求 **qǐqiú** to beseech

11. 不允 **bùyǔn** to not permit

12. 甘心 **gānxīn** to resign oneself to, to accept willingly

13. 乔装打扮 **qiáozhuāng dǎbàn** to disguise

14. 游走 **yóuzǒu** itinerant

15. 算命先生 **suànmìng xiānsheng** fortune teller

16. 卦 **guà** fortune-telling symbols

为了嘉奖她卓越的领导能力，皇帝任命她为将军。花木兰以年迈的父母需要照顾为由婉拒了。一群战友依依不舍，护送花木兰返乡。那时，木兰进入了内屋，出来时成了飒爽女子，令战友们惊讶又开怀。

　　"梁祝"的故事和花木兰的传说在中国可谓家喻户晓。古往今来，它们以各种各样的文学和戏剧形式展现给世人。由此我们推测，在中国传统文化对女性严苛的束缚之下，一直涌动着一股"女权意识"的暗流，即承认男人能做的事情，女人也一样做得到。同时，"梁祝"的悲剧也可以被视为对社会风俗的无声抗议，是世间男女渴望追求一生真爱的见证。

17. 令爱 **lìng'ài** (your) beloved daughter

18. 忍心 **rěnxīn** to have the heart to

19. 女扮男装 **nǚbàn nánzhuāng** (a woman) to dress up as a man

20. 面相 **miànxiàng** facial features

21. 不情愿 **bùqíngyuàn** grudgingly

22. 吩咐 **fēnfù** to instruct, to order

23. 侍女 **shìnǚ** maidservant

24. 书童 **shūtóng** student

25. 出嫁 **chūjià** (a woman) to get married

26. 相见恨晚 **xiāngjiàn hènwǎn** to be sorry for not having met sooner

27. 结下金兰之好 **jiéxià jīnlán zhīhǎo** to become sworn brothers

28. 同窗共读 **tóngchuāng gòngdú** to be classmates (by the same window)

29. 情同手足 **qíng tóng shǒuzú** intimate (feeling like hands and feet of the same person)

30. 同床共眠 **tóngchuáng gòngmián** to share the same bed

31. 家境 **jiājìng** family background

32. 永结同心 **yǒngjié tóngxīn** to tie the knot

33. 白头偕老 **báitóu xiélǎo** to grow old together

34. 暗示 **ànshì** to hint

35. 反应 **fǎnyìng** reaction

36. 调侃 **tiáokǎn** to tease

37. 举止 **jǔzhǐ** mannerisms

38. 朝夕相处 **zhāoxī xiāngchǔ** to be together morning and evening

39. 催 **cuī** to rush (someone)

40. 信守承诺 **xìnshǒu chéngnuò** to abide by a promise

41. 心生一计 **xīnshēng yíjì** to come up with a scheme

42. 提亲 **tíqīn** to propose marriage

43. 贫寒 **pínhán** poor

44. 体面 **tǐmiàn** decent, respectable

45. 聘礼 **pìnlǐ** bride present

46. 许配 **xǔpèi** to betroth

47. 名门望族 **míngmén wàngzú** a prominent family

48. 亲事 **qīnshì** marriage

49. 期盼 **qīpàn** to look forward to

50. 重逢 **chóngféng** reunion

51. 订婚 **dìnghūn** to get engaged

52. 永别 **yǒngbié** final farewell

53. 伤心欲绝 **shāngxīn yùjué** utterly heartbroken

54. 泪流满面 **lèiliú mǎnmiàn** face covered with tears

55. 誓言 **shìyán** to swear, to make an oath

56. 至死不渝 **zhìsǐ bùyú** will not change until death

57. 生不能同衾，死也要同穴 **shēng bùnéng tóngqīn, sǐ yěyào tóngxué** if we can't share the same quilt in life, then we will share a grave in death

58. 朝廷 **cháotíng** court

59. 任命 **rènmìng** to appoint

60. 县令 **xiànlìng** county magistrate

61. 晋升官职 **jìnshēng guānzhí** to be promoted to an official position

62. 荣耀 **róngyào** glory

63. 解脱 **jiětuō** to be extricated from

64. 遵照 **zūnzhào** to comply with

65. 遗愿 **yíyuàn** last wish (of a dying person)

66. 葬 **zàng** to bury

67. 坟墓 **fénmù** grave

68. 花轿 **huājiào** sedan chair

69. 暴风雨 **bàofēngyǔ** thunderstorm

70. 躲避 **duǒbì** to dodge

71. 闪电 **shǎndiàn** lightning

72. 震耳欲聋 **zhèn'ěr yùlóng** deafening

73. 炸雷 **zhàléi** explosive thunder

74. 电闪雷鸣 **diànshǎn léimíng** thunder and lightning

75. 裂开 **lièkāi** to split open

76. 纵身一跃 **zòngshēn yíyuè** to leap

77. 彩虹 **cǎihóng** rainbow

78. 裂缝 **lièfèng** crack

79. 蝴蝶 **húdié** butterfly

80. 翩翩起舞 **piānpiān qǐwǔ** to flutter and dance

81. 据称 **jùchēng** allegedly

82. 取材于 **qǔcáiyú** to take its material from, to be based on

83. 虚构 **xūgòu** imaginary, fabricated

84. 就 **jiù** with regards to

85. 搜索 **sōusuǒ** to search

86. 数不胜数 **shǔ búshèng shǔ** countless

87. 担当 **dāndāng** to undertake, to assume (a role),

88. 角色 **juésè** role

89. 案例 **ànlì** case

90. 无从知晓 **wúcóng zhīxiǎo** no way to know

91. 凭借 **píngjiè** by virtue of...

92. 下···围棋 **xià...wéiqí** to play Go (a brain-taxing board game)

93. 结交 **jiéjiāo** to befriend

94. 文人墨客 **wénrén mòkè** literati

95. 举荐 **jǔjiàn** to recommend

96. 辞官 **cíguān** to resign from an official position

97. 挽留 **wǎnliú** to retain

98. 朔方 **shuòfāng** the North

99. 兵马使 **bīngmǎshǐ** military official

100. 接替 **jiētì** to succeed (a position)

101. 暴露 **bàolù** to expose

102. 游历四方 **yóulì sìfāng** to travel around

103. 知州 **zhīzhōu** provincial governor

104. 才华 **cáihuá** literary or artistic talent

105. 女婿 **nǚxù** son-in-law

106. 受宠若惊 **shòuchǒng ruòjīng** overwhelmed by an unexpected favor

107. 坦言 **tǎnyán** to speak frankly

108. 性别 **xìngbié** gender

109. 辞 **cí** to resign (from a post)

110. 俸禄 **fènglù** stipend

111. 擅长 **shàncháng** to excel in

112. 比武 **bǐwǔ** martial arts competition

113. 选拔 **xuǎnbá** selection

114. 犯···之罪 **fàn...zhī zuì** to commit the crime of...

115. 欺君 **qījūn** to deceive the emperor

116. 斩首 **zhǎnshǒu** to be beheaded

117. 临死不惧 **línsǐ bújù** fearless in face of death

118. 慷慨陈词 **kāngkǎi chéncí** to present one's views fervently

119. 欣赏 **xīnshǎng** to appreciate

120. 赐予 **cìyǔ** to bestow on

121. 状元 **zhuàngyuán** to be the best in an imperial exam

122. 要数 **yàoshǔ** to reckon to be

123. 游牧部落 **yóumù bùluò** nomadic tribe

124. 侵扰 **qīnrǎo** to invade and harrass

125. 招兵 **zhāobīng** to recruit soldiers

126. 壮丁 **zhuàngdīng** able-bodied men

127. 年事已高 **niánshì yǐgāo** to be advanced in age

128. 应征入伍 **yìngzhēng rùwǔ** to respond to a draft and join the ranks

129. 并肩作战 **bìngjiān zuòzhàn** to fight shoulder-to-shoulder

130. 嘉奖 **jiājiǎng** to commend

131. 卓越 **zhuóyuè** outstanding

132. 将军 **jiāngjūn** general

133. 以···为由 **yǐ...wéiyóu** on the grounds of...

134. 婉拒 **wǎnjù** to tactfully decline

135. 依依不舍 **yīyī bùshě** reluctant to part with (someone)

136. 返乡 **fǎnxiāng** to return home

137. 飒爽 **sàshuǎng** valiant

138. 开怀 **kāihuái** happy

139. 可谓 **kěwèi** can be said to be

140. 家喻户晓 **jiāyù hùxiǎo** known to every household

141. 展现 **zhǎnxiàn** to present, to show

142. 推测 **tuīcè** to surmise

143. 严苛 **yánkē** harsh

144. 束缚 **shùfù** fetters, restrictions

145. 涌动 **yǒngdòng** to gush, to well up

146. 女权意识 **nǚquán yìshí** feminist consciousness

147. 暗流 **ànliú** undercurrent

148. 无声抗议 **wúshēng kàngyì** silent protest

149. 见证 **jiànzhèng** testimony

fn1. 盛世 **shèngshì** prosperous, flourishing

fn2. 成就卓著 **chéngjiù zhuózhù** to be outstanding in achievements

Questions for contemplation and discussion

1. The story about Liang Shanbo and Zhu Yingtai has been designated by China's State Council as a national "intangible cultural heritage." What are the merits of this story that make it worthy of this designation?

2. Literary scholars have called this story China's "Romeo and Juliet." What are the similarities and differences between these two works?

3. Can you think of cases of women disguised as men or vice-versa in Western culture?

4. Do you think marriages that result from romantic love are more successful than those arranged by parents in premodern times?

5. What do you know about the practice of parents helping young people find a spouse in contemporary China? How is this different from premodern times?

A Young Widow's Sorrow

The Great Wall of China as we know it today was built over the course of two millennia. As one of the New Seven Wonders of the World, it is naturally a source of pride to the nation, but the Chinese people also remember the sorrow of those who were sacrificed in the process of building it.

孟姜女哭长城

闻名中外的长城是在两千年的历史长河中分阶段修建起来的。作为世界七大奇观之一，长城自然成为了中华文明的骄傲，但中国人也会铭记在修建长城的过程中贫苦百姓被逼得家破人亡的悲惨故事。

When the first emperor of China founded the Qin Dynasty in 221 BCE, one of his major projects was to link the existing walls built by preceding nation-states into one Great Wall. To accomplish this, the emperor amassed a huge amount of manpower through forced labor.

One day, when a young lady by the name of Meng-Jiang was sewing in the courtyard of her home, she heard a rustling noise under the bushes. She was startled to find a young man hiding there. As she was about to scream, he motioned her to be quiet, and told her in a whisper, "The emperor's soldiers knocked on my family's gate. I managed to escape through the back door. A lot of men have already been drafted to work on the Great Wall. Some of them have died from hunger or exhaustion. I'm a scholar and wouldn't be of much use for this kind of work anyway. By the way, my name is Fan Xiliang." At that, Meng-Jiang realized that he must be the son of the kindly elderly couple named Fan. As Xiliang came out from the bushes, Meng-Jiang noticed his handsome features and the same gracious dignified manner of his parents. She went inside and persuaded her parents to shelter Xiliang for the time being. But before long, the pair fell in love, and soon both sets of parents gave their blessing for them to be married.

Unbeknownst to Xiliang, there was a good-for-nothing fellow who had his eye on Meng-Jiang for quite some time, but her parents firmly rejected his repeated proposals to marry her. When he heard that Xiliang had just married Meng-Jiang, he reported Xiliang's whereabouts to the authorities. On the third day after the wedding, when the young couple were still immersed in their honeymoon, the emperor's soldiers burst through the gate and grabbed Xiliang. When Meng-Jiang rushed toward her husband, a soldier pushed her aside, leaving her stunned as she watched her husband being dragged away.

The season changed from spring to summer, then from summer to fall, and Meng-Jiang still had no news of her husband. With winter approaching, Meng-Jiang worried that the clothes Xiliang had with him

秦始皇在公元前221年建立秦朝后，力主的一项重大工程就是将春秋战国时期各地修建的城墙连接起来，成为一座完整的长城。为了实现这个宏愿，他从各地抓来大批壮丁服苦役。

有一天，名叫孟姜的年轻女子在自家院子里做针线活，突然听见灌木丛里一阵窸窸窣窣的声响，随后惊讶地发现里面藏着一个年轻小生。她刚要喊叫，小生示意她别出声，并悄悄地告诉她："皇家士兵在敲我们家大门的时候，我从后门逃走了。很多男人都被抓去修长城了，有的已经饿死累死了。我是个书生，根本不会做那样的活儿。对了，我叫范喜良…。"孟姜这才明白他一定是慈祥的范老夫妇家公子。喜良从灌木丛里走出来后，孟姜看到喜良面目英俊，神情像他父母一样又有尊严又和蔼可亲。孟姜走进屋里，说服父母暂时收留了喜良。不久，两人就相爱了，双方的父母也很赞成他们二人喜结连理。

喜良不知道，有个无赖早就看上了孟姜，多次来求婚，都被孟姜父母回绝了。无赖听说喜良刚娶了孟姜，就向衙门告发了他。婚礼后的第三天，小两口还沉浸在幸福的蜜月中，皇家士兵突然破门而入，抓住了喜良。孟姜不顾一切地冲向丈夫，却被士兵推到了一边，她又惊又气，也只能眼睁睁地看着丈夫被拉出了家门。

春去夏来，夏去秋来，孟姜还是没有丈夫的消息。眼看冬天快要到了，孟姜担心喜良身上穿的衣服不足以御寒，

would not be adequate to keep him warm. She quickly sewed some cotton-padded clothes and set out to find her husband at the Great Wall. After half a month on the road, she finally saw a row of worksites, each of them building a section of the Great Wall. She went from one worksite to another, asking if anyone knew the whereabouts of Fan Xiliang. Finally, she found a laborer who said he knew Xiliang, but had not seen him in the last few days. At this news, Meng-Jiang thought her heart would burst. But a few moments later, someone else said that Xiliang had died a couple of days earlier and was buried under a new section of the Great Wall. This tragic news hit Meng-Jiang like a thunderbolt! She fell to her knees, tears streaming down her face. For three days and three nights, she knelt sobbing near the spot where Xiliang was buried. Her untold grief moved heaven and earth; the sky grew dark, the wind started howling, then with a huge thunderclap the section of the wall in front of Meng-Jiang collapsed, exposing Fan Xiliang's remains. She finally saw her husband, but he would never see her again. Slowly she wiped away her last tears, then tenderly dressed her husband's remains in the padded clothes she had made and prepared to take him home for a proper funeral.

As she started on her journey, the Qin emperor arrived with his entourage to inspect the Great Wall. Catching sight of the sad but beautiful young widow, he suddenly thought of a plan to make her his concubine. This outrageous proposal from the emperor triggered an astonishing reaction: Meng-Jiang first felt her grief turn into anger, then her anger turn into courage! At that moment, she only wanted to humiliate this despicable emperor and bring dignity and respect to her husband's soul. With perfect composure, she replied, "Yes, I will be your concubine, but only if you help put my husband to rest by doing these three things: build a long causeway by the sea; at the end of the causeway build a grave mound for my husband; then personally conduct a memorial ceremony to honor my husband."

就赶紧做了几件棉衣，出发去长城寻找丈夫了。走了半个多月，她终于看见一排长长的劳役工地，每个点都在修筑一段长城。她从一个点走到下一个点，一路打听有没有人知道范喜良的下落。终于，有个民工说他认识喜良，不过好几天没看见他了。孟姜听了又欣喜又忐忑。过了一会儿，有人说喜良几天前刚死了，被埋在一段新修筑的长城下面了。这个噩耗对孟姜来说就像晴天霹雳一样！她顿时跪倒在地上，泪如雨下。她跪在喜良被埋葬的地方，哭了三天三夜。她无尽的悲伤感动了天地，顿时，乌云翻滚，狂风呼啸，只听一声巨雷，孟姜面前的一段长城崩塌了，露出了范喜良的尸骨。孟姜终于看见了丈夫，但他却再也看不到她了。孟姜慢慢地擦干了眼泪，轻轻地把亲手做的棉衣给丈夫穿上，准备把他带回家去好好地安葬。

　　就在孟姜踏上回家之路的时候，秦始皇率领随从来到长城巡视。看到这位悲伤又美丽的年轻寡妇，皇帝突然萌生了要娶她为妃子的念头。皇帝的非分要求令孟姜的心绪由悲恸转为愤怒，继而转化为勇气！那一刻，她只想羞辱这个无耻的皇帝，为丈夫的在天之灵带来尊严。于是，孟姜镇定自若地告诉皇上："好的，如果皇上答应我三件事，让我的亡夫之灵得以安息，我就愿意做皇上的妃子。第一件是在海边修一条长堤；第二件是在长堤的尽头为我亡夫修一座坟；最后一件是皇上要亲自祭奠我的亡夫。"

The besotted emperor agreed to these three conditions and rushed to get them done. As he completed the memorial ceremony, he turned to Meng-Jiang to claim his prize. What he received instead was her final rebuke: "Despicable despot! You have no mercy for your people! Your tyranny killed my husband! And now you are a fool to think that I would be your concubine!" With that, Meng-Jiang grabbed her husband's remains and leaped into the embrace of the sea.

Commentary

The legend of Lady Meng-Jiang has gone through several variations over the last two thousand years. It originated from a true historical event that predates the unification of China and the building of the Great Wall. In 550 BCE the aggressive king of Qi (in present-day Shandong Province) attacked two neighboring states to the west and vanquished them. As his victorious troops were returning home the following year, the king suddenly ordered them to make a surprise attack on the state of Ju to the south. The Qi general Qi Liang was killed in battle. As the defeated Qi troops were carrying their general's funeral bier back to the capital, Linzi, Qi Liang's wife journeyed halfway to meet them. The king sent a messenger to the outskirts of the capital to convey his condolences. To Qi Liang's wife, this was a terrible insult to her husband who had given his life to his country. She rejected the king's messenger and demanded that the king himself conduct a dignified funeral within the capital and build a proper grave in the suburb. We can see Qi Liang's grave in Linzi today only because this widow in mourning had the courage to confront a powerful king.

痴情的皇上满口答应了孟姜的三个条件，而且赶紧把三件事都做完了。当他完成祭奠仪式，转过头来看着孟姜，想要搂她入怀时，只见孟姜大声地呵斥道："卑鄙的暴君！你对百姓没有一丁点慈悲怜悯！你的暴政杀了我丈夫！还以为我会愿意做你的妃子，真是愚蠢！"说完，孟姜抱起丈夫的遗体，纵身跳进了大海。

评论

孟姜女的传说经历了两千多年的演变。故事的雏形起源于秦朝统一中国并修建长城以前的一个真实历史事件。公元前550年，雄心勃勃的齐王（齐国在今山东省）攻打西边的两个邻国，并征服了它们。第二年，在军队凯旋而归的途中，齐王忽然下令突袭南边的莒国。齐国大将杞梁阵亡。当战败的齐国将士抬着杞梁的灵柩返回京城临淄的途中，杞梁妻到半路去迎接，齐王派一个下属到京城郊外去吊唁。在杞梁妻看来，丈夫为国捐躯，君王却派人来郊外吊唁是对死者的不尊重，因此要求齐王亲自在京城内举行祭奠仪式，并将杞梁安葬在京城郊区。由于杞梁妻不惧君王，敢于维护丈夫的勇气，时至今日，临淄还能看到杞梁墓。

Documentation of the above event in the *Zuo Zhuan*, a late fourth century Chinese narrative history, contained a sparse outline of the event, but it tapped into a major vein of popular discontent at different points in Chinese history and left plenty of room for the imagination of later historians and writers. The contemporary version, in which Meng-Jiang is the heroine, was created during the Ming Dynasty. Having successfully overthrown the Yuan Dynasty and chased the defeated Mongols back to Mongolia, the Ming emperors embarked on a major reconstruction of the Great Wall to keep the nomads to the north at bay. The enormous cost and loss of lives resulting from this project aroused tremendous popular resentment. In traditional Chinese society where open protest was highly risky, writers became adept at using the tool of allegory. Chinese historiography has traditionally portrayed the first emperor of the Qin Dynasty as a brutal tyrant, capable of burning the classics and burying Confucian scholars alive. Since the original Great Wall was also attributed to him, writers in the Ming Dynasty found in him the perfect allegorical protagonist for the legend of Lady Meng-Jiang. Thus, this story set in the Qin Dynasty was of great political relevance in the Ming Dynasty.

Although the reader may have the impression that the Qin emperor in this legend was a total villain, he was in fact a much more complex and controversial figure. Undoubtedly, he governed ruthlessly, but we should also recognize his achievements, including the standardization of weights and measures, the axle lengths of carts, various laws, and the writing system. In 1987 his tomb was designated a UNESCO World Heritage site, and it has yielded thousands of terracotta soldiers and horses, some of which have been displayed in museums around the world.

To this day, the legend of Lady Meng-Jiang remains beloved by the Chinese people. It also received official blessing from China's State Council in 2006, when it was among the four love stories designated as "intangible cultural heritage."

《左传》里记载的上述事件只是一个梗概，却切中了中国历史上不同时期百姓内心不满的要害，因此为后世的文史学家留下了丰富的想象空间。以孟姜女为女主人公的现代版故事创作于明朝。明朝廷推翻了元朝并将蒙古人赶回蒙古以后，开始大兴土木，修建长城以抵御北方的游牧民族。重修长城造成人力物力的巨大损耗在民间引起了强烈的愤慨。在中国传统的社会，公开抗争会带来极大的风险，因此作家们都很善于运用寓言故事来表达心中的不满。由于秦始皇下令焚书坑儒，在中国历史上被视为一个残忍的暴君，并且也是第一个修建长城的皇帝，他很自然地被明代作家们选为了孟姜女传说中的反面人物。由此看来，这个以秦朝为历史背景的故事在明朝具有重要的政治意义。

关于秦始皇，这篇传说故事也许会给读者留下一个片面的印象，即他是个彻头彻尾的恶棍。实际上，秦始皇是一个多面复杂又有争议的历史人物。不可否认，秦始皇执政时残酷无情，但也取得了重要的成就，包括统一了度量衡、车轴长度、法律以及文字。秦始皇陵墓出土了上千件兵马俑，其中一些曾在世界各地的博物馆展出。1987年，秦始皇陵墓被联合国教科文组织列为了世界文化遗产。

时至今日，孟姜女的传说故事在中国家喻户晓。2006年，中国国务院把四个民间爱情故事列入了国家级非物质文化遗产名录，其中之一就是孟姜女哭长城。

Vocabulary

1. 闻名中外 **wénmíng Zhōng-wài** famous in China and abroad

2. 分阶段 **fēnjiēduàn** in stages

3. 奇观 **qíguān** amazing sight, wonder

4. 骄傲 **jiāo'ào** pride

5. 铭记 **míngjì** to remember always; engraved in memory

6. 家破人亡 **jiāpò rénwáng** family broken and people perished

7. 悲惨 **bēicǎn** tragic

8. 力主 **lìzhǔ** to advocate

9. 宏愿 **hóngyuàn** grand ambition

10. 壮丁 **zhuàngdīng** strong man

11. 服苦役 **fú kǔyì** to serve hard labor

12. 针线活 **zhēnxiànhuó** needlework

13. 灌木 **guànmù** shrub

14. 窸窸窣窣 **xīxīsūsū** shish-shish (onomatopoeia)

15. 小生 **xiǎoshēng** young man

16. 示意 **shìyì** to signal

17. 书生 **shūshēng** scholar

18. 慈祥 **cíxiáng** kindly

19. 公子 **gōngzǐ** son

20. 面目英俊 **miànmù yīngjùn** handsome

21. 神情 **shénqíng** expression

22. 和蔼可亲 **hé'ǎi kěqīn** kind and amiable

23. 喜结连理 **xǐjié liánlǐ** to tie the knot

24. 无赖 **wúlài** rascal

25. 求婚 **qiúhūn** to propose marriage

26. 回绝 **huíjué** to refuse

27. 衙门 **yámén** government office

28. 告发 **gàofā** to inform against

29. 沉浸 **chénjìn** to immerse

30. 蜜月 **mìyuè** honeymoon

31. 破门而入 **pòmén érrù** to break in

32. 眼睁睁 **yǎnzhēngzhēng** to watch helplessly (eyes wide open)

33. 御寒 **yùhán** to protect against the cold

34. 劳役工地 **láoyì gōngdì** work site

35. 修筑 **xiūzhù** to build

36. 下落 **xiàluò** whereabouts

37. 忐忑 **tǎntè** "heart going up and down," anxious

38. 噩耗 **èhào** tragic news

39. 晴天霹雳 **qíngtiān pīlì** a bolt out of the blue

40. 跪倒 **guìdǎo** to fall on one's knees

41. 埋葬 **máizàng** to bury (a dead person)

42. 顿时 **dùnshí** suddenly

43. 乌云翻滚 **wūyún fāngǔn** dark clouds rolling

44. 狂风呼啸 **kuángfēng hūxiào** wind howling

45. 巨雷 **jùléi** giant thunder

46. 崩塌 **bēngtā** to collapse

47. 露出 **lùchū** to expose

48. 尸骨 **shīgǔ** corpse

49. 擦干 **cāgān** to wipe dry

50. 安葬 **ānzàng** to hold a proper burial

51. 率领随从 **shuàilǐng suícóng** to lead an entourage

52. 巡视 **xúnshì** to make an inspection tour

53. 寡妇 **guǎfù** widow

54. 萌生 **méngshēng** to sprout

55. 妃子 **fēizi** concubine

56. 非分 **fēifèn** presumptuous, preposterous

57. 心绪 **xīnxù** mood, state of mind

58. 悲恸 **bēitòng** grief

59. 愤怒 **fènnù** anger

60. 继而 **jìér** then

61. 羞辱 **xiūrǔ** to humiliate

62. 无耻 **wúchǐ** shameless

63. 在天之灵 **zàitiān zhī líng** spirit in heaven, departed soul

64. 镇定自若 **zhèndìng zìruò** calm and composed

65. 亡夫 **wángfū** deceased husband

66. 安息 **ānxī** to rest in peace

67. 长堤 **chángdī** causeway

68. 坟 **fén** grave

69. 祭奠 **jìdiàn** to pay homage

70. 痴情 **chīqíng** infatuation

71. 仪式 **yíshì** ceremony

72. 搂···入怀 **lǒu...rùhuái** to embrace

73. 呵斥 **hēchì** to scold

74. 卑鄙 **bēibǐ** despicable

75. 暴君 **bàojūn** tyrant

76. 慈悲怜悯 **cíbēi liánmǐn** compassion

77. 愚蠢 **yúchǔn** foolish, stupid

78. 遗体 **yítǐ** remains (of deceased person)

79. 纵身 **zòngshēn** to plunge oneself into

80. 演变 **yǎnbiàn** to evolve

81. 雏形 **chúxíng** prototype, embryonic form

82. 雄心勃勃 **xióngxīn bóbó** ambitious

83. 凯旋而归 **kǎixuán érguī** to return triumphantly (from war)

84. 突袭 **tūxí** to raid

85. 阵亡 **zhènwáng** to be killed in action

86. 灵柩 **língjiù** coffin

87. 吊唁 **diàoyàn** to condole

88. 为国捐躯 **wèiguó juānqū** to die for one's country

89. 不惧 **bújù** fearless

90. 维护 **wéihù** to defend, to uphold

91. 梗概 **gěnggài** broad outline

92. 切中···要害 **qièzhòng...yàohài** to hit the nail on the head

93. 现代版 **xiàndàibǎn** contemporary version

94. 大兴土木 **dàxīng tǔmù** to launch a big construction

95. 抵御 **dǐyù** to defend against

96. 损耗 **sǔnhào** to cause loss and waste

97. 愤慨 **fènkǎi** indignation

98. 抗争 **kàngzhēng** to protest

99. 善于 **shànyú** to be good at

100. 寓言 **yùyán** allegory

101. 焚书坑儒 **fénshū kēngrú** to burn books and bury scholars

102. 片面 **piànmiàn** one-sided

103. 彻头彻尾 **chètóu chèwěi** downright, through and through

104. 恶棍 **ègùn** scoundrel

105. 有争议 **yǒu zhēngyì** controversial

106. 不可否认 **bùkě fǒurèn** undeniable

107. 执政 **zhízhèng** to be in power

108. 残酷无情 **cánkù wúqíng** cruel and merciless

109. 度量衡 **dùliànghéng** weights and measures

110. 车轴长度 **chēzhóu chángdù** axle length

111. 陵墓 **língmù** tomb

112. 兵马俑 **bīngmǎyǒng** terracotta soldiers and horses

113. 联合国教科文组织 **Liánhéguó Jiàokēwén Zǔzhī** UNESCO (United Nations Education Science and Culture Organization)

114. 遗产 **yíchǎn** heritage

115. 家喻户晓 **jiāyù hùxiǎo** household name, known to every family

116. 非物质文化遗产 **fēiwùzhì wénhuà yíchǎn** intangible cultural heritage

Questions for contemplation and discussion

1. In your opinion, what makes the legend of Lady Meng-Jiang worthy of being named an intangible cultural heritage?

2. Why do you think the Great Wall was declared one of the New Seven Wonders of the World? Has this story changed your previous understanding of the Great Wall?

3. Given that the legend of Lady Meng-Jiang evolved from the true story of the wife of General Qi Liang around 550 BCE, what elements were added by the creators of the legend, and what is the significance of each addition?

4. Do you see any similarities between this story and the "Butterfly Dream"? Are these similarities due to coincidence or to the use of tropes (literary devices)?

5. Can you think of another literary work from any culture in the world that is a political allegory?

Judge Bao Takes On the Emperor's Son-in-Law

During the Northern Song Dynasty (960–1127), there was a three-generation provincial family with a husband and wife—Chen Shimei and Qin Xianglian, their young son and daughter, and Chen's elderly parents. Shimei aspired to be a scholar and eventually pass the civil service exam to become an official. Xianglian supported him by taking on the burden of being the family's breadwinner on top of all the usual housework. The family barely scraped by, but they felt content and secure knowing that better days were ahead. Shimen's parents felt blessed to have such a loving and capable daughter-in-law, and their days were further brightened by their two smart and well-behaved grandchildren.

包公怒斩陈世美

北宋时期(960年–1127年)，河南陈家庄有一户三代同堂的人家，夫妻二人名叫陈世美与秦香莲，有一双年幼的儿女，还有世美年迈的父母。世美一心向学，盼望着将来金榜题名，进京做官。香莲全心全意地支持丈夫，除了承担全部家务活儿，养家糊口也得靠她。一家人勉强度日，但想到日子有盼头，也很知足了。世美的父母有这么一位能干贤惠的儿媳妇，再加上两个聪明乖巧孙儿女，也十分欣慰。到了世美进

When it came time for Shimei to go to the capital Kaifeng to take the civil service exam, Xianglian made him a handsome outfit and sent him off looking like an elegant scholar.

No one expected Shimei to lose touch with his family once he left home. Things began to get tough for the family in the second year when the province suffered a drought that brought on a famine. This natural disaster continued into the third year, and Shimei's elderly parents eventually died of starvation. With nowhere to turn, Xianglian decided to take her children to Kaifeng to find out what had happened to Shimei during the last three years.

Meanwhile, Shimei had taken the civil service exam and in fact, had been placed first on that exam. The emperor was so impressed that he summoned Shimei to court and offered him the hand of his daughter in marriage. Shimei was flabbergasted by the offer, but being a sharp-minded fellow he decided to tell the emperor that he had been orphaned as a child, had no family whatsoever, and therefore would be supremely honored to join the royal family.

Upon arriving in Kaifeng, Xianglian immediately inquired if anyone had heard of her husband Chen Shimei. By then, the emperor's new son-in-law had become the talk of the town. Xianglian could not believe what people told her. At first, she was ecstatic that her husband was alive and well, then she was alarmed at realizing what this meant for her and her children. Finally, she told herself that the emperor's son-in-law could not possibly be the same Chen Shimei as her husband. The only way to be sure was to go to the princess's mansion and see with her own eyes.

The next morning Xianglian took her children to the princess's mansion. When she told the gateman that they were the family of Chen Shimei, the gateman thought she must be some crazy woman trying to extort money. Hearing the commotion at the gate, Chen Shimei came out to see what was going on. The two children, seeing their father for the first time in three years, started calling "Baba! Baba!" Shimei's face

京赶考的日子，他穿上香莲亲手缝制的新衣，看上去一副儒雅书生的模样，上路往开封府去了。

谁也没想到，世美一出门就和家里断了联系。第二年，家乡大旱，发生了饥荒，他们一家人的日子过得很艰难。这场天灾持续到了第三年，世美的父母最终饿死了。香莲走投无路，决定带着孩子去开封府寻找丈夫，好歹查明过去三年世美到底在做什么。

实际上，世美参加了科举考试，并中了状元。皇帝很欣赏这个年轻人，就招他进宫，想把自己的女儿许配给他。世美听了皇上的话懵了一下，但他很聪明，立刻编了一套谎话，告诉皇上他自幼成为了孤儿，无家可归，能成为驸马是他今生莫大的荣幸。

香莲一到开封府就四处打听丈夫的下落。那个时候，皇上新招的驸马早就成了大街小巷里人们热议的话题。香莲简直不敢相信这个消息是真的。知道丈夫安然无恙，她先是欣喜万分，继而想到失去了丈夫，又十分惶恐。最后她安慰自己，皇上的驸马跟自己的丈夫不可能是同一个人，也许是同名同姓，但能把事情弄清楚的唯一办法就是去公主府亲眼看一看。

第二天早上，香莲带着两个孩子到了公主府。香莲告诉门卫她和孩子是陈世美的家人，门卫以为香莲一定是来敲诈勒索的疯女人。听到大门口有动静，世美就出来看看究竟发生了什么事儿。三年没见到父亲的两个孩子一见到陈世美出

immediately turned dark as he ignored his family and yelled at the gateman to shoo the three vagrants away and shut the gate.

That day, as Xianglian and the two children wandered dejectedly in the capital, a kindly minister by the name of Wang Yanling caught sight of them and knew instinctively that they had been abused. After hearing Xianglian's story, he came up with a scheme to awaken Chen Shimei's conscience. The next day was Shimei's birthday and Minister Wang had been invited to the party. He proposed to bring Xianglian disguised as a ballad singer to entertain the guests. At the party Xianglian played the *pipa* as she sang a ballad about a forsaken wife. Shimei recognized not only Xianglian but also the story to be his own. The ballad was so moving that almost everyone at the party had tears in their eyes. But Shimei only seethed with anger, and even clashed with Minister Wang. When he called some guards to drag Xianglian away, Minister Wang followed and urged her to file a suit against Shimei with Judge Bao. He then handed her his folding fan to help her gain access to the judge.[1] Chen Shimei, realizing he was in serious trouble, told his palace guard Han Qi that Xianglian was a swindler out to blackmail him. He ordered Han to kill Xianglian and the two children that night, thereby eliminating all witnesses.

That night Han Qi found Xianglian and her children sheltering in an old temple. After hearing Xianglian's story, he realized that he had been duped by Chen, and that Chen was intent on murdering his own wife and children! Unable to carry out Chen's order and fearing punishment, Han Qi slit his own throat instead. Shocked and angered by Shimei's atrocity, Xianglian took Han's bloody sword as further evidence to use in court.

---

[1] The folding fan is a well-known prop used in Chinese opera to represent various things. Here it functions like a modern-day calling card.

来，就大声叫到："爸爸，爸爸!"世美顿时变了脸色，根本不理会家人，大声地叫门卫赶走那三个叫花子，关上大门。

那天，香莲和两个孩子孤苦伶仃地流浪在京城的大街上，正好被心地善良的大臣王延龄看在了眼里，他立刻意识到这娘仨受到了欺辱。听完了香莲的叙述后，王延龄想出了一个唤醒陈世美良心的计策。第二天是陈世美的生日，王大臣已经受邀出席。他让香莲扮成卖唱女，随他一同进宫，在寿宴上卖唱。香莲弹着琵琶，唱了一曲妻子被抛弃的辛酸歌谣。世美不但认出了香莲，而且明白香莲唱的负心郎就是他本人。几乎所有人都被这首歌谣打动了，只有世美怒火中烧，甚至与王大臣起了争执。世美叫来了下人，将香莲拽出了宫门。王大臣跟了出来，将自己的一把白纸折扇交给了香莲[1]，并嘱咐她到包公处状告陈世美。世美知道自己处境不妙，于是对自己的宫中侍卫韩祺谎称香莲是一个来敲诈他的骗子，命令韩祺当晚杀了香莲和两个孩子，实际上就是要杀人灭口。

那天晚上，韩祺在一座古庙里找到了香莲和两个孩子。听了香莲的叙述，韩祺才意识到陈世美不但谎话连篇，而且要杀妻灭子! 韩祺左右为难，他不忍心杀了香莲母子，但又担心自己抗命会受到惩罚，于是拔剑自刎。香莲对世美的诡计又震惊又愤怒，将韩祺带血的剑收好，作为庭审时候的物证。

---

[1] 折扇是中国戏曲中常用的道具之一，具有多种用途。这里的作用相当于现代人的名片。

Judge Bao had hoped that Chen Shimei would come to his senses and admit the truth so that he could impose a reasonable penalty. But Chen Shimei was certain that no judge, not even the "iron-faced" impartial Judge Bao, would dare touch the emperor's son-in-law, so he flatly denied any wrongdoing. This left the judge with no choice but to call Xianglian to testify. With Han Qi's sword in hand, and looking straight into her husband's eyes, Xianglian accused him of abandoning his parents, disavowing his wife and children, and attempting to murder her and the children. To this list Judge Bao added a fourth crime—deceiving the emperor, for which the penalty was death. When Chen still showed no sign of repentance, Judge Bao ordered the executioners to rip off Chen's dragon robe and tie him up. Alarmed by this turn of events, Chen's retainers rushed back to the princess's mansion to call for help.

In no time the princess and the queen mother arrived. The two immediately ordered Judge Bao to release Chen Shimei, and the queen mother reminded him that the penalty for defying an imperial order was death. The princess, realizing that the two children were indeed Chen Shimei's, demanded that Xianglian turn them over to her! At that moment, not even Judge Bao could stand up to the queen mother, so he handed Xianglian three hundred taels of silver and urged her to return home and raise her children in peace.

To the judge's surprise, Xianglian spurned the compensation, saying that as long as Shimei was alive he would find a way to eliminate her and the children. She then lashed out at the judge for being a spineless lackey to the high and mighty. Her words triggered a sense of shame in the judge and reignited his resolve to do justice, even knowing that he would be sacked and may well be executed. To make his defiance clear to the queen mother, he turned to her and said, "If I am to be executed, it will be after the faithless husband Chen Shimei has been executed!" Then, to demonstrate his willingness to sacrifice his career in the name of justice, he removed his official cap, the insignia of his judgeship. Fi-

包公原本希望陈世美能够良心发现，承认事实，他就可以酌情判罚。然而陈世美确信没有任何法官，哪怕是铁面无私的包公，敢动他驸马爷的一根毫毛，所以他拒不认错。包公别无选择，只好升堂，传香莲上堂作证。香莲手握韩祺带血的剑，直视世美的眼睛，控诉他丢下父母不管，抛妻弃子，还企图杀人灭口。除此之外，包公还指责世美犯了欺君的死罪。世美依然毫无悔过之意，包公便下令刽子手脱下世美的龙袍，将他捆绑起来。世美的随从见势不好，赶紧回公主府去搬救兵。

不一会儿，公主和太后都赶来了。两人命令包公立即放了陈世美，太后还提醒包公违抗圣旨就是死罪。公主意识到两个孩子确实是陈世美的孩子，就要求香莲把孩子交给她！那一刻，连包公也拗不过太后，所以他取了三百两银子递给香莲，劝她回家去好好养育儿女。

出乎包公的意料，香莲拒收银两，并表示只要世美还活着，他就会想办法杀了她和孩子。随即，香莲指责包公官官相护，胆小怕事。包公听了香莲的话，羞愧难当，决定即使自己丢官也要为香莲伸冤。为了向太后表明抗旨的决心，包公转向她说："如果我将被处死，那也要在这个忘恩负义的陈世美之后！"为了表明他"宁丢官职，也要公正无私"，包公

nally, he ordered the executioners to take the emperor's son-in-law to the guillotine. As justice was served, there was nothing the princess or the queen mother could do but watch in horror.

Afterword: The role of the emperor's son-in-law

Throughout much of Chinese history, the best way for a commoner to rise in society was to pass the civil service exam and be recruited into the government bureaucracy. Does Chen Shimei becoming the emperor's son-in-law fit this narrative? And why would an emperor choose a commoner rather than an aristocrat to be his son-in-law? The answer lies in the word for the emperor's son-in-law—*fùmǎ*—which literally means "auxiliary horse." The regular Chinese word for son-in-law is *nǚxù*, so why would the emperor's son-in-law be called an "auxiliary horse" instead? The mystery goes back to the relationship between the first emperor of the Qin Dynasty and his son-in-law.

The king of Qin, who was to become the first emperor, survived two assassination attempts before he conquered all the other states. After he became emperor, he narrowly escaped a third attempt. During his reign as emperor (221–210 BCE), he made frequent tours of his empire, always accompanied by a sizable entourage. On one of those tours, as he passed a mountain pass, an enormous metal cone rolled down the mountain, barely missed his carriage although it shattered the carriage in front of his. From then on, he expanded his fleet of carriages, rode in a different one each time, and even positioned a decoy of himself in another carriage. In most cases the decoy would be his son-in-law. That is how the decoy riding in an auxiliary horse-drawn carriage—the "auxiliary horse"—became the term for the emperor's son-in-law.

Chinese history is strewn with assassination attempts on emperors, so it is no wonder they were vigilant to the point of being paranoid about

取下了象征自己官职的乌纱帽。最后，他下令刽子手将驸马爷送上断头台。正义最终得到了伸张，公主和太后也无可奈何，只能惊恐地看着正在发生的一切。

附录：驸马爷的角色

在中国历史长河的大部分时间里，平民在社会上提升地位的最佳途径就是通过科举考试，进官府做官。陈世美通过科举被钦定为驸马是否算是一个典型呢？为什么皇帝会选择平民而不是名门望族的公子作为驸马呢？答案就在于"驸马"这个词，字面的意思就是"辅助的马"。"女儿的丈夫"在中文里的常用词是"女婿"，那为什么皇帝的女婿被叫做"辅助的马"呢？这个谜可以追溯到秦始皇与其女婿之间的关系。

秦国的国君在统一中国成为秦始皇之前，遭遇了两次未遂刺杀。成为秦始皇以后，他差一点在第三次刺杀中毙命。在秦始皇统治期间(公元前221年－公元前210年)，他往往带着大批随从到各地巡游。有一次，当他的大队人马经过一座山口时，山上滚下来一个巨大的铁锤，将他前面的一辆马车砸烂了，而秦始皇侥幸保住了性命。从那以后，秦始皇扩充了皇家车马队，每次出巡都坐一辆不同的马车，并且在另一辆马车里安排一名替身。在大多情况下，这名替身便是他的女婿。因此，辅助马车里的替身，也就是"驸马"就成为了皇帝女婿的称谓。

中国历史上企图刺杀皇帝的事件数不胜数，难怪皇帝们严加防范，甚至因此有了疑心病。秦始皇之后，皇帝的女婿

it. It is unknown whether emperors' sons-in-law continued to serve as decoys for possible assassinations, but the term "auxiliary horse" that originated from the assassination attempt on the first emperor has stuck. What we do know is that the men handpicked by emperors to be their sons-in-law were typically deployed in some "auxiliary" function in personal service to the royal family, something less glorious than being a government official. The scholars who distinguished themselves in the civil service exam were the best minds of the land and would typically be deployed in functions that required a high level of intellect. When Chen Shimei was offered the position of "auxiliary horse," he was guaranteed a life of luxury and leisure but not a career that he had aspired to, and certainly not what his wife had sacrificed for.

Vocabulary

1. 怒斩 **nùzhǎn** to execute in anger

2. 三代同堂 **sāndài tóngtáng** three generations under one roof

3. 年幼 **niányòu** young in age

4. 年迈 **niánmài** advanced in age

5. 一心向学 **yìxīn xiàngxué** to be dedicated to learning

6. 金榜题名 **jīnbǎng tímíng** to pass the imperial exam (lit. to be listed on the "golden list of names)

7. 养家糊口 **yǎngjiā húkǒu** to be breadwinner for the family

8. 勉强度日 **miǎnqiǎng dùrì** to get by barely

9. 有盼头 **yǒu pàntou** to have a future to look forward to

10. 知足 **zhīzú** to be content

11. 能干贤惠 **nénggàn xiánhuì** capable and virtuous

12. 乖巧 **guāiqiǎo** well-behaved and bright

13. 欣慰 **xīnwèi** gratified

14. 赶考 **gǎnkǎo** to take the (imperial) exam

15. 缝制 **féngzhì** to sew and make

16. 儒雅书生 **rúyǎ shūshēng** elegant scholar

17. 模样 **múyàng** appearance

18. 大旱 **dàhàn** severe drought

是否继续扮演替身的角色，我们不得而知，但源自企图刺杀秦始皇时候的"驸马"一词流传了下来。实际上，皇帝亲手挑选的女婿往往在皇室里承担"辅助"作用，料理一些私事，而不是担当显耀的公职。在科举考试中脱颖而出的书生大多是全国最优秀的人才，通常都会被委以重任。当陈世美被选为"驸马"时，他得以一生享受荣华富贵，但实际上与他原先的抱负相违背，更辜负了香莲为之付出的巨大牺牲。

19. 饥荒 **jīhuāng** famine

20. 天灾 **tiānzāi** natural disaster

21. 走投无路 **zǒutóu wúlù** to have no way to turn

22. 好歹 **hǎodǎi** for better or worse

23. 科举考试 **kējǔ kǎoshì** imperial exam (for civil service)

24. 中了状元 **zhòngle…zhuàngyuán** to be the top winner in an exam, to be the valedictorian

25. 欣赏 **xīnshǎng** to appreciate, to admire

26. 许配 **xǔpèi** to betroth

27. 懵 **měng** baffled, freaked out

28. 编···谎话 **biān...huǎnghuà** to fabricate a lie

29. 自幼 **zìyòu** since childhood

30. 孤儿 **gūér** orphan

31. 无家可归 **wújiā kěguī** homeless

32. 驸马 **fùmǎ** son-in-law of the emperor

33. 莫大 **mòdà** the greatest (lit. none greater)

34. 荣幸 **róngxìng** honor and good fortune

35. 打听···下落 **dǎting...xiàluò** to inquire about the whereabouts of...

36. 大街小巷 **dàjiē xiǎoxiàng** streets and alleys

37. 安然无恙 **ānrán wúyàng** safe and sound

38. 欣喜万分 **xīnxǐ wànfēn** overjoyed

39. 继而 **jìér** and then (i.e. immediately following)

40. 惶恐 **huángkǒng** to panic

41. 安慰 **ānwèi** to console

42. 门卫 **ménwèi** doorman, gate guard

43. 敲诈勒索 **qiāozhà lèsuǒ** to extort

44. 动静 **dòngjìng** movements, commotion

45. 究竟 **jiūjìng** after all; what it's all about

46. 顿时 **dùnshí** suddenly, immediately

47. 理会 **lǐhuì** to acknowledge, to take note of

48. 叫花子 **jiàohuāzi** beggar

49. 孤苦伶仃 **gūkǔ língdīng** forlorn

50. 流浪 **liúlàng** to wander around

51. 心地善良 **xīndì shànliáng** kind-hearted

52. 欺辱 **qīrǔ** to bully, to abuse

53. 叙述 **xùshù** narrative

54. 唤醒…良心 **huànxǐng...liángxīn** to awaken (someone's) conscience

55. 计策 **jìcè** plan, scheme

56. 受邀出席 **shòuyāo chūxí** to accept an invitation to attend

57. 卖唱女 **màichàngnǚ** itinerant singer (female)

58. 寿宴 **shòuyàn** birthday banquet

59. 琵琶 **pípá** lute

60. 抛弃 **pāoqì** to abandon

61. 辛酸 **xīnsuān** bitter, heart-wrenching

62. 负心郎 **fùxīnláng** unfaithful man, heartbreaker

63. 打动 **dǎdòng** to sway, to move (emotions)

64. 怒火中烧 **nùhuǒzhōngshāo** to burn with anger

65. 争执 **zhēngzhí** to dispute

66. 拽 **zhuài** to drag

67. 折扇 **zhéshàn** folding fan

68. 嘱咐 **zhǔfù** to enjoin

69. 状告 **zhuànggào** to sue

70. 处境不妙 **chǔjìng búmiào** in a bad fix, in dire straits

71. 侍卫 **shìwèi** bodyguard

72. 谎称 **huǎngchēng** to lie saying...

73. 骗子 **piànzi** fraudster, swindler

74. 杀人灭口 **shārén mièkǒu** to murder in order to destroy a witness

75. 谎话连篇 **huǎnghuà liánpiān** lies upon lies

76. 左右为难 **zuǒyòu wéinán** between a rock and a hard place

77. 不忍心 **bùrěnxīn** to not have the heart to...

78. 抗命 **kàngmìng** to disobey an order

79. 惩罚 **chéngfá** punishment

80. 拔剑自刎 **bájiàn zìwěn** to draw a sword and commit suicide

81. 诡计 **guǐjì** a heinous scheme

82. 庭审 **tíngshěn** court trial

83. 物证 **wùzhèng** material evidence

84. 良心发现 **liángxīn fāxiàn** awakening of one's conscience

85. 酌情判罚 **zhuóqíng pànfá** to order a discretionary penalty

86. 哪怕 **nǎpà** even if

87. 铁面无私 **tiěmiàn wúsī** scrupulously fair and judicious

88. 动···一根毫毛 **dòng...yìgēn háomáo** to touch a tiny hair of...

89. 升堂 **shēngtáng** to conduct trial (lit. to ascend to a hall)

90. 传···上堂 **chuán...shàngtáng** to summon...to court

91. 作证 **zuòzhèng** to testify

92. 控诉 **kòngsù** to accuse (in court)

93. 抛妻弃子 **pāoqī qìzǐ** to abandon one's wife and children

94. 企图 **qǐtú** to attempt to...

95. 指责 **zhǐzé** to accuse

96. 犯···死罪 **fàn...sǐzuì** to commit a capital crime

97. 欺君 **qījūn** to deceive a ruler

98. 悔过 **huǐguò** to repent

99. 刽子手 **guìzishǒu** executioner

100. 龙袍 **lóngpáo** dragon robe

101. 捆绑 **kǔnbǎng** to tie up

102. 随从 **suícóng** follower, underling

103. 见势不好 **jiànshì bùhǎo** to see a bad situation coming on

104. 搬救兵 **bān jiùbīng** to call for reinforcements

105. 违抗圣旨 **wéikàng shèngzhǐ** to disobey an imperial order

106. 拗不过 **niùbúguò** unable to bring someone around

107. 出乎⋯意料 **chūhū...yìliào** unexpected by..., to so-and-so's surprise

108. 官官相护 **guānguān xiānghù** officials protecting each other

109. 胆小怕事 **dǎnxiǎo pàshì** intimidated by possible trouble

110. 羞愧难当 **xiūkuì nándāng** to be unbearably ashamed

111. 伸冤 **shēnyuān** to vindicate

112. 抗旨 **kàngzhǐ** to resist an order

113. 处死 **chǔsǐ** to put to death

114. 忘恩负义 **wàng'ēn fùyì** ungrateful

115. 宁⋯也要 **nìng...yěyào...** must...even if...

116. 象征 **xiàngzhēng** to symbolize

117. 乌纱帽 **wūshāmào** black hat (of government officials)

118. 断头台 **duàntóutái** guillotine

119. 伸张 **shēnzhāng** to uphold (justice)

120. 无可奈何 **wúkě nàihé** helpless, have no way out

121. 惊恐 **jīngkǒng** frightened

122. 途径 **tújìng** path

123. 钦定 **qīndìng** to determine (by the emperor)

124. 典型 **diǎnxíng** typical

125. 名门望族 **míngmén wàngzú** noble family

126. 谜 **mí** puzzle

127. 追溯 **zhuīsù** to trace back

128. 遭遇 **zāoyù** to encounter (a disaster)

129. 未遂 **wèisuì** to fail in an attempt

130. 刺杀 **cìshā** to assassinate

131. 毙命 **bìmìng** to meet a violent death

132. 巡游 **xúnyóu** to make an inspection tour

133. 铁锤 **tiěchuí** iron hammer

134. 砸烂 **zálàn** to smash to bits

135. 侥幸 **jiǎoxìng** fortunately, by sheer luck

136. 扩充 **kuòchōng** to expand

137. 替身 **tìshēn** stand-in, surrogate

138. 称谓 **chēngwèi** title, appellation

139. 数不胜数 **shǔ búshèng shǔ** countless

140. 严加防范 **yánjiā fángfàn** to enact strict precautions

141. 疑心病 **yíxīnbìng** paranoia, hypochondria

142. 扮演···的角色 **bànyǎn...de juésè** to play the role of...

143. 不得而知 **bùdé ér zhī** unable to know

144. 源自 **yuánzì** to originate from

145. 流传 **liúchuán** to pass down, to disseminate

146. 料理 **liàolǐ** to manage

147. 显耀 **xiǎnyào** glorious

148. 公职 **gōngzhí** public office

149. 脱颖而出 **tuōyǐng ér chū** to pull ahead, to come to the fore

150. 委以重任 **wěi yǐ zhòngrèn** to entrust with important tasks

151. 荣华富贵 **rónghuá fùguì** honor and wealth

152. 抱负 **bàofù** ambition, aspiration

153. 违背 **wéibèi** to go against

154. 辜负 **gūfù** to fail to live up to

fn. 道具 **dàojù** stage prop

Questions for contemplation and discussion

1. Write an epilogue to this story by creating an outcome for all the characters in the story after Chen Shimei was executed.

2. The Judge Bao series of 100 court cases has been popular in China since it was first published during the Ming Dynasty, even inspiring performing arts. What is the appeal of this judge that gives the series such staying power?

3. Do you know of another story from China or elsewhere in the world with the theme of a successful husband abandoning the wife who has persevered through good times as well as bad with him? Does this happen in real life?

4. How common are assassinations of emperors or presidents? Can you talk about some cases that you know of?

5. In your opinion, are there any similarities between the civil service exam in imperial China and the modern-day Chinese college entrance exam? What are the obvious differences?

The Ten Trials of a Taoist Sage

During the late Tang Dynasty (618–906 CE) in the provincial town of Handan, a dejected man by the name of Lü Dongbin was walking into a wineshop. He had just resigned his position in the corrupt government bureaucracy and needed solace. At the entrance he met an old man who introduced himself as the Taoist sage Zhongli Quan. When Master Zhongli heard Dongbin tell about his recent plight, he realized that this was an old soul who could become a sage, so he invited Dongbin to his humble home for a simple supper of millet porridge. As the porridge was cooking, Dongbin dozed off and had the following dream:

> He excelled in the imperial exam and received a civil service position. He rose quickly up the ranks and eventually became the prime minister. Meanwhile, he married the daughter of an aristocratic family and had two children. However, his success aroused the jealousy of his peers, who then maligned him. The emperor stripped him of his office and banished him to the frontiers. His wife betrayed him, he lost all this wealth, and his children were killed by bandits.

钟离权十考吕洞宾

唐朝末年（618年－906年），在省城邯郸，一个<u>垂头丧气</u>的男人走进了一家<u>酒铺</u>。此人名叫吕洞宾，刚从<u>腐败</u>的<u>衙门</u>辞了<u>官职</u>，便来酒铺<u>解闷</u>。他刚进门，就遇见一位气度非凡的老人，自称<u>道士</u>钟离权。道士了解了洞宾的<u>困境</u>之后，就知道与面前这位先生有缘，愿意<u>点化</u>他，于是邀请他到自己的<u>寒舍</u>去共享简单的<u>黄粱粥</u>。黄粱刚下锅不久，洞宾就<u>打起了瞌睡</u>，进入了<u>梦乡</u>：

在梦里，他在<u>科举</u>考试中成绩<u>优异</u>，并得到了一个<u>文官</u>的职位。他<u>步步高升</u>，最终成了一国<u>宰相</u>。同时，他娶了一位<u>世家千金</u>，养育了两个孩子。然而，他的<u>功名</u>成就引起了同行的<u>嫉妒</u>，于是他们就<u>诋毁</u>他。皇帝撤了他的官职，并将他<u>流放</u>到了<u>边疆</u>。他的妻子<u>背叛</u>了他，孩子也被<u>土匪</u>杀害了，他失去了所有的<u>财富</u>，变得<u>一无所有</u>了。

Fortunately, Dongbin was "saved" by waking up from the dream. He had dozed off for only twenty minutes, but the dream had played out eighteen years of his spectacular rise and fall! Still groggy, he heard Master Zhongli say, "I see your dream finished just as the millet is ready." Dongbin was surprised that the master seemed to know he had a dream. It was, in fact, the master who had staged the dream to help Dongbin renounce his desire for glory and wealth in the transient world. Master Zhongli knew that he had accomplished this when Dongbin pleaded to become his disciple. The master was secretly delighted, but first he wanted Dongbin to prove himself to be a worthy disciple by going through the following ten trials:

　　这时候，洞宾一下子从梦中惊醒了过来。他只小睡了二十分钟，却在梦里经历了十八年跌宕起伏的人生！昏昏沉沉中，他听见道士对他说："粥快好了，你也梦醒了。"动宾很惊讶，道士如何知道他做了梦？原来，道士是为了帮助洞宾断绝对尘世荣华富贵的欲念才呈现了那个梦境。当洞宾恳求道士收他为徒的时候，道士明白他希望点化洞宾的意愿已经达成了。道士心中暗喜，不过他仍希望洞宾能够证明自己是一个值得他点化的徒弟，所以就决定要十考洞宾：

1. When Dongbin returned home from a trip one day, he found his entire family had died of illness. Knowing that their time in this world had ended, he calmly prepared their bodies to return to earth. When they suddenly came back to life, he realized that he had passed the first trial.

2. Dongbin took some surplus produce to sell at the market. After a buyer bargained for a price and collected the goods, he reneged and only wanted to pay half. Dongbin kindly returned the half payment to the buyer and walked home contented.

3. When a beggar came to Dongbin's door on New Year's Day, Dongbin gave him a generous amount, but the beggar kept asking for more, and then started yelling at Dongbin for being too slow. Dongbin just bowed to the beggar and apologized. The beggar left with a smile.

4. Dongbin was grazing his flock of sheep in the hills when suddenly a tiger charged at the sheep. He hurried to the front of the flock, knowing that he may become the tiger's meal. The tiger just walked away.

5. Dongbin was studying in a hut in the mountains. When dusk came, a lovely young lady knocked on the door, seeking shelter for the night. Dongbin welcomed her in and both of them settled down for the night. In the middle of the night, the lady started seducing him, but he remained as calm as still water until daylight, when it was time for the lady to go on her way.

6. One day, returning home from a trip, Dongbin found that his home had been ransacked by thieves. Every sellable thing was gone, and he was left with no means to live. Calmly, he took a hoe to dig for medicinal plants to sell. Unintentionally, he dug up a pile of gold. Thinking that someone must have hidden it there, he quickly reburied the gold and left.

1. 有一天，洞宾出远门归来，发现全家人都病死了。他知道亲人们在这个尘世已经走到了<u>尽头</u>，就平静地准备<u>安葬</u>他们。突然，亲人们都<u>苏醒</u>过来了，洞宾知道他通过了第一考。

2. 洞宾带了一些<u>富余</u>的农产品到集市去卖。一个人讲好了价钱，拿了东西之后，又<u>反悔</u>了，只愿意付一半的价钱。洞宾很客气地把他已付的一半也退还给了他，<u>自己心满意足</u>地回家了。

3. 有个<u>乞丐</u>在大年初一来到洞宾家门口，洞宾<u>慷慨解囊</u>，给了他一大笔钱，但乞丐还要更多的钱，甚至开口骂洞宾动作太慢了。洞宾只向乞丐<u>作揖</u>道歉。乞丐笑着离开了。

4. 洞宾正在山上放羊，突然一只老虎<u>扑向</u>羊群。他明知自己可能被老虎吃掉，但还是<u>健步</u>跑到了羊群的前面，但老虎却走开了。

5. 洞宾在山里的一间小<u>茅屋</u>里读书。<u>黄昏</u>时分，一个年轻漂亮的女子敲门，<u>要借宿</u>一晚。洞宾请女子进了屋，两人就在一个屋里<u>安寝</u>了。谁知这女子半夜里不<u>安分</u>起来，百般<u>挑逗</u>洞宾，但他<u>心如止水</u>，<u>丝毫不理</u>会女子。天亮后，女子便上路了。

6. 有一天，洞宾出门回来，发现家里被<u>盗贼洗劫一空</u>。能卖的东西都被偷了，他的生活也没了<u>着落</u>。洞宾<u>一声不吭</u>，拿起<u>锄</u>头去挖药材来卖钱。<u>无意间</u>，他挖到了一堆金子。猜想金子一定是有人<u>藏</u>在那里的，他赶紧把金子<u>原封不动</u>地重新埋了起来，然后离开了。

7. One day Dongbin bought several copper utensils. When he got home, he discovered that they were actually made of gold. Thinking that the shopkeeper must have made a mistake, he hurriedly returned them to the shop.

8. A deranged monk was hawking some medicine in the marketplace, calling out, "Whoever takes this medicine will die and be reborn as a saint." Who would dare buy such medicine? For a fortnight, the monk failed to sell any of his medicine. Dongbin decided to help this monk even though he did not believe what the monk claimed the medicine would do. He bought some of the medicine and took it. Sure enough, nothing happened to him.

9. In mid-spring, when the river swelled from melted snow, Dongbin was gliding down the river in his flimsy boat when a storm suddenly whipped up, with fierce winds and strong currents. Knowing that he could be sucked into a whirlpool at any moment, he sat calmly like a speck on a leaf. In due course, the storm blew over and he floated to shore.

10. Dongbin was home alone one day when suddenly a pack of demons came to attack him. When he did not flinch, they quietly went away. Then came a pack of hideous monsters dragging a bloody convict toward him. The convict yelled at Dongbin, "You killed me in your previous reincarnation, now it's time for retribution!" Dongbin accepted his fate and went to get some rope and a knife to kill himself. Suddenly, he heard a loud shout. The convict disappeared and someone clapping his hands descended in front of Dongbin. It was Master Zhongli!

7. 有一天，洞宾买了几件铜器。到家后，他发现这些器具实际上是黄金材质的。心想店主一定是弄错了，洞宾连忙把这些器具退给了店主。

8. 一个疯狂的僧人在集市上兜售一种药，他大声吆喝道："谁吃了这种药，会死后重生，成为圣人。"谁敢买这样的药呢？僧人吆喝了两个星期，也没有一个人买他的药。洞宾决定帮一帮僧人，但他不相信那种药有僧人所说的药效。洞宾买了一些服用了。果然，他安然无事。

9. 仲春时节，积雪开始融化，河水也上涨了，洞宾划着一叶小舟顺河而下。突然，一场暴风雨来了，河面上掀起了狂风巨浪。洞宾知道自己随时有可能落入漩涡中，但他平静地坐在小舟上。等暴风雨过去了，他也平安地漂到了岸边。

10. 有一天，洞宾独自在家里。突然，一群恶魔闯进来攻击他。洞宾很淡定，恶魔就悄悄地离开了。接着一群面目狰狞的怪物拖着一个血淋淋的罪犯朝他走来。罪犯对洞宾大吼大叫道："你上辈子杀了我，现在得偿命！"洞宾认命了，去拿绳子和刀，准备自杀。突然，他听到有人大叫一声，罪犯不见了，有人从天而降，拍着手站到了他面前，是钟离道士！

The master was the first to speak: "A worldly heart is hard to extinguish, a sagely soul is hard to find! Your eagerness to find a master is exceeded by my eagerness to find a worthy disciple! Now that you have passed the ten trials, you will no doubt become a Taoist saint. But you still need to fulfill your earthly mission of good deeds to humankind. I will teach you the technique of turning ordinary metal into gold and silver, with which you will relieve the suffering of mortals on earth. Once you have completed three thousand good deeds, I will return to transform you into an immortal."

Dongbin hesitated a moment before he asked, "Would the gold and silver produced by this technique change in the future?"

The master replied, "Yes, it will revert to its original element after three thousand years."

Dongbin quickly said, "Then this is going to ruin people in three thousand years! I would never do that!"

Hearing this, the master let out a big chuckle and said, "Your supreme benevolence has already earned your three thousand good deeds!"

From that point on, Dongbin continued to cultivate himself under the guidance of Master Zhongli and went on to do countless good deeds on earth before he became an immortal.

道士开口说道："尘心难灭，仙才难得！你求师心切，而我寻高徒的愿望更甚！如今你通过了十考，无疑将来会成为道家圣人。只不过你在尘世的功德善行还未圆满。我要教给你点铁成金银之术，你便可以救济世人。待你三千功德圆满之后，我再来度你成仙。"

洞宾犹豫了片刻，问道："点出来的金银将来还会变吗？"

道士答道："会的，三千年后金银都会变回原形。"

洞宾连忙说："那会毁了三千年后的人啊，我绝不会做那样的事情！"

道士听了，哈哈大笑道："你的大慈大悲已经抵得了三千善行了！"

从此以后，洞宾在钟离道士的引导下不断修行，在人间行善无数，最终成了仙人。

Afterword

This story is obviously a legend. However, there was in fact an official by the name of Lü Dongbin in the early ninth century, when the Tang Dynasty had declined, and the central government was in disarray. Lü came from a long line of government officials, so naturally he aspired to uphold his family tradition. However, he failed the civil service exam several times. He eventually passed the exam and served as a county magistrate. Soon he became disillusioned with officialdom and abandoned his position to become a recluse. While he was not a successful bureaucrat, he was well-respected as a poet. The *Complete Tang Poems* compiled in the Qing Dynasty includes 106 poems by him.

Given the nature of legends, it is hard to determine exactly when and how they were created. However, in the case of Lü Dongbin, the legend most likely originated from the "All-True" School of Taoism that was founded around 1170,[1] more than three centuries after the real-life Lü Dongbin. In this school of Taoism, Zhongli Quan and Lü Dongbin are revered as two of the five northern progenitors of Taoism. In Chinese folk culture, the two are better known as two of the "Eight Immortals."

According to Taoism, official life is anathema to being a spiritual person. What made Lü Dongbin such a good candidate for Taoist sainthood was that he renounced his life as an official. This Taoist streak may have resided in him even before he became an official. The name he was given at birth was Lü Yan, *yán* meaning "cliff." At some point, he gave himself the name *Dòngbīn*, meaning "guest of the cave." Perhaps this is a sign that he was already envisioning himself as a recluse living in a cave.

---

[1] This was during the Southern Song Dynasty. However, the All-True School of Taoism was founded in the northern territory that was wrested from the Song in 1127 by the Jurchens, who proclaimed themselves the Jin Dynasty.

附 录

很显然，上面的故事是一个传说。然而，在公元九世纪初，唐朝没落，朝廷陷入混乱的时期，确实有一位名叫吕洞宾的官员。他出生在官宦世家，自然渴望继承家风。不过，他考了好几次科举都没考中，后来终于通过了考试，当了县令。不久，他便对官场大失所望，于是弃官当了隐士。虽然他官场失意，但却是一位备受尊敬的诗人。清代编纂的《全唐诗》收录了他的106首诗。

一般来说，很难确定一个传说故事是何时，又是如何创造出来的。然而，吕洞宾的传说很有可能源于公元1170年左右创建的"全真"道教[1]，比真实生活中的吕洞宾晚了三个多世纪。在全真教中，钟离权和吕洞宾被尊为道教北五祖中的两位仙人。在中国民间文化中，他们两位也是百姓熟知的"八仙"中的两位。

道家认为，一个超凡脱俗的人自然会憎恶官场生活。吕洞宾之所以成为道家圣人的最佳人选正是因为他摈弃了官职。这样的道家情怀或许在他做官以前就根植于心了。洞宾出生时，家人给他取名吕岩，岩的意思是"悬崖"。后来，他给自己起了洞宾的字，即"山洞里的宾客"。这或许表明他已经把自己想象成一个身居山洞里的隐士了。

---

[1] 从时间上来看是南宋时期。然而，自称为金朝的女真人在1127年从宋朝手中夺取了北方领土，而道教的全真教派正是在金朝的这个地区兴起的。

Vocabulary

1. 垂头丧气 **chuítóu sàngqì** dejected (head hanging spirit depleted)

2. 酒铺 **jiǔpù** wine shop

3. 腐败 **fǔbài** corrupt

4. 衙门 **yámén** government office

5. 辞···官职 **cí...guānzhí** to resign from office

6. 解闷 **jiěmèn** to relieve ennui

7. 气度非凡 **qìdù fēifán** to exude an extraordinary spirit

8. 道士 **dàoshì** Taoist

9. 困境 **kùnjìng** predicament

10. 点化 **diǎnhuà** to enlighten

11. 寒舍 **hánshè** humble abode

12. 黄粱粥 **huángliáng zhōu** millet porridge

13. 打···瞌睡 **dǎ...kēshuì** to doze off

14. 梦乡 **mèngxiāng** dreamland

15. 科举 **kējǔ** imperial exam

16. 优异 **yōuyì** excellent

17. 文官 **wénguān** civil servant

18. 步步高升 **bùbù gāoshēng** to rise in rank step by step

19. 宰相 **zǎixiàng** prime minister

20. 世家千金 **shìjiā qiānjīn** daughter of a prominent family

21. 功名 **gōngmíng** fame

22. 嫉妒 **jídù** envy

23. 诋毁 **dǐhuǐ** to slander

24. 撤 **chè** to dismiss (from office)

25. 流放 **liúfàng** to exile

26. 边疆 **biānjiāng** frontier

27. 背叛 **bèipàn** to betray

28. 土匪 **tǔfěi** bandit

29. 财富 **cáifù** wealth

30. 一无所有 **yì wú suǒ yǒu** to have nothing, destitute

31. 惊醒 **jīngxǐng** to awake with a start

32. 跌宕起伏 **diēdàng qǐfú** to go through ups and downs

33. 断绝 **duànjué** to break off

34. 尘世荣华富贵 **chénshì rónghuá fùguì** worldly glory and wealth

35. 欲念 **yùniàn** desire

36. 恳求 **kěnqiú** to plead

37. 收···为徒 **shōu...wéi tú** to accept...as a disciple

38. 暗喜 **ànxǐ** to be secretly happy

39. 尽头 **jìntóu** the end (of the road)

40. 安葬 **ānzàng** to bury (and put to peace)

41. 苏醒 **sūxǐng** to awake

42. 富余 **fùyú** surplus

43. 反悔 **fǎnhuǐ** to regret

44. 心满意足 **xīnmǎn yìzú** totally content

45. 乞丐 **qǐgài** beggar

46. 慷慨解囊 **kāngkǎi jiěnáng** to generously open one's pocket

47. 作揖 **zuòyī** to make a bow

48. 扑向 **pūxiàng** to pounce on

49. 健步 **jiànbù** to walk or jump briskly

50. 茅屋 **máowū** cottage

51. 黄昏 **huánghūn** sunset

52. 借宿 **jièsù** to stay overnight

53. 安寝 **ānqǐn** to settle down to sleep

54. 安分 **ānfèn** to keep oneself within proper bounds

55. 挑逗 **tiǎodòu** to tease, to tantalize

56. 心如止水 **xīnrú zhǐshuǐ** heart like still water, totally unmoved

57. 丝毫 **sīháo** slightest

58. 理会 **lǐhuì** to pay attention to, to take notice of

59. 盗贼 **dàozéi** thief

60. 洗劫一空 **xǐjié yìkōng** ransacked

61. 着落 **zhuóluò** a way out of difficulties

62. 一声不吭 **yìshēng bùkēng** to not make a sound, to keep silent

63. 锄头 **chútou** hoe

64. 无意间 **wúyìjiān** inadvertently, unintentionally

65. 藏 **cáng** to hide

66. 原封不动 **yuánfēng búdòng** intact, without touching the original seal

67. 铜器 **tóngqì** bronze or copper utensil

68. 材质 **cáizhì** material

69. 僧人 **sēngrén** monk

70. 兜售 **dōushòu** to hawk

71. 吆喝 **yāohe** to call out

72. 死后重生 **sǐhòu chóngshēng** to be reborn after death

73. 圣人 **shèngrén** saint

74. 药效 **yàoxiào** drug effect

75. 服用 **fúyòng** to take (medication)

76. 安然无事 **ānrán wúshì** safe and sound

77. 仲春 **zhòngchūn** mid spring

78. 融化 **rónghuà** to melt

79. 一叶小舟 **yíyè xiǎozhōu** a small boat

80. 掀起···狂风巨浪 **xiānqǐ... kuángfēng jùlàng** to whip up a big wind and great waves

81. 漩涡 **xuánwō** whirlpool

82. 恶魔 **èmó** demon

83. 淡定 **dàndìng** calm

84. 面目狰狞 **miànmù zhēngníng** hideous face, vile visage

85. 血淋淋 **xiělínlín** bloody

86. 罪犯 **zuìfàn** criminal

87. 偿命 **chángmìng** to repay a life with a life

88. 认命 **rènmìng** to accept fate

89. 从天而降 **cóng tiān ér jiàng** to descend from the sky

90. 尘心难灭 **chénxīn nánmiè** a dusty heart (worldly concerns) dies hard

91. 仙才难得 **xiāncái nándé** material for sainthood is rare

92. 求师心切 **qiúshī xīnqiè** eager to find a mentor

93. 寻高徒 **xún gāotú** to search for a superior disciple

94. 更甚 **gèngshèn** even greater

95. 无疑 **wúyí** undoubtedly

96. 功德善行 **gōngdé shànxíng** good deeds

97. 点铁成金银之术 **diǎntiě chéng jīnyín zhī shù** technique for turning iron into gold and silver

98. 救济 **jiùjì** to relieve (human suffering)

99. 度···成仙 **dù...chéngxiān** to transcend into an immortal

100. 犹豫 **yóuyù** to hesitate

101. 毁 **huǐ** to destroy

102. 大慈大悲 **dàcí dàbēi** great compassion

103. 抵得了 **dǐdeliǎo** to be worth

104. 修行 **xiūxíng** to practice or cultivate (spirituality)

105. 行善 **xíngshàn** to do good deeds

106. 没落 **mòluò** to be in decline

107. 陷入 **xiànrù** to fall into

108. 官宦世家 **guānhuàn shìjiā** official family

109. 继承家风 **jìchéng jiāfēng** to carry on the family tradition

110. 考中 **kǎozhòng** to pass an exam (for admission)

111. 县令 **xiànlìng** county magistrate

112. 大失所望 **dàshī suǒwàng** to be greatly disappointed

113. 弃官 **qìguān** to abandon an official post

114. 隐士 **yǐnshì** recluse

115. 失意 **shīyì** thwarted, disappointed

116. 编纂 **biānzuǎn** to compile and edit

117. 源于··· **yuányú...** to originate from...

118. 北五祖 **Běi Wǔzǔ** Northern Five Patriarchs (Taoism)

119. 超凡脱俗 **chāofán tuōsú** otherworldly, above the ordinary

120. 憎恶 **zēngwù** to detest

121. 之所以···是因为··· **zhī suǒyǐ...shì yīnwèi...** the reason...is because...

122. 人选 **rénxuǎn** candidate

123. 摈弃 **bìnqì** to abandon

124. 情怀 **qínghuái** sentiment, mindset

125. 根植于心 **gēn zhí yú xīn** to take root in the heart

126. 悬崖 **xuányá** cliff

127. 宾客 **bīnkè** guest

fn. 女真 **Nǚzhēn** Jurchens

uestions for contemplation and discussion

1. What did the "millet dream" clarify for Lü Dongbin? Have you ever had a dream that gave you a valuable message?

2. Choose five trials out of the ten, and tell what human characteristic is being tested by each of your chosen trials.

3. What does this story tell you about the attitude toward officialdom in popular Chinese culture?

4. Have you heard of the set phrase "dog bites Lü Dongbin, does not recognize the good heart 狗咬吕洞宾，不识好人心" or "the eight immortals cross the sea, each showing their special ingenuity 八仙过海，各显神通"? If not, look them up or ask a Chinese friend. Can you describe a situation when one of these phrases can be used?

5. In your opinion are certain people born with an innate temperament or karma that makes them inclined toward enlightenment?

"Books to Span the East and West"

Tuttle Publishing was founded in 1832 in the small New England town of Rutland, Vermont [USA]. Our core values remain as strong today as they were then—to publish best-in-class books which bring people together one page at a time. In 1948, we established a publishing outpost in Japan—and Tuttle is now a leader in publishing English-language books about the arts, languages and cultures of Asia. The world has become a much smaller place today and Asia's economic and cultural influence has grown. Yet the need for meaningful dialogue and information about this diverse region has never been greater. Over the past seven decades, Tuttle has published thousands of books on subjects ranging from martial arts and paper crafts to language learning and literature—and our talented authors, illustrators, designers and photographers have won many prestigious awards. We welcome you to explore the wealth of information available on Asia at www.tuttlepublishing.com.

Published by Tuttle Publishing, an imprint of Periplus Editions (HK) Ltd.

www.tuttlepublishing.com

Copyright © 2024 by Vivian Ling and Wang Peng

Cover image © comuseum.com

Library of Congress Control Number: 2024931228

ISBN 978-0-8048-5728-4

First edition
28 27 26 25 24
10 9 8 7 6 5 4 3 2 1   2403CM
Printed in China

Distributed by

North America, Latin America & Europe
Tuttle Publishing
364 Innovation Drive, North Clarendon
VT 05759-9436 U.S.A.
Tel: 1 (802) 773-8930 Fax: 1 (802) 773-6993
info@tuttlepublishing.com
www.tuttlepublishing.com

Japan
Tuttle Publishing
Yaekari Building 3rd Floor
5-4-12 Osaki Shinagawa-ku, Tokyo 141 0032
Tel: (81) 3 5437-0171 Fax: (81) 3 5437-0755
sales@tuttle.co.jp
www.tuttle.co.jp

Asia Pacific
Berkeley Books Pte. Ltd.
3 Kallang Sector #04-01, Singapore 349278
Tel: (65) 6741-2178 Fax: (65) 6741-2179
inquiries@periplus.com.sg
www.tuttlepublishing.com

TUTTLE PUBLISHING® is a registered trademark of Tuttle Publishing, a division of Periplus Editions (HK) Ltd.